LITTLE MEN

OF THE NFL

Action-packed profiles of pro football's little men: Pat Fischer, Harold Jackson, Floyd Little, Fran Tarkenton, Randy Vataha, Nemiah Wilson, and Garo Yepremian. With speed, courage, and determination, they made a big mark in the NFL.

LITTLE
MEN
OF THE NFL

BY BOB RUBIN

Illustrated with photographs

RANDOM HOUSE · NEW YORK

PHOTOGRAPH CREDITS: Vernon J. Biever, 13, 33; Malcolm Emmons, 4, 17, 21, 133; Emmons & Brockway, 68; Fred Roe, 6, 118; United Press International, endpapers, 2, 24, 30, 39, 47, 50, 61, 65, 72, 81, 85, 93, 103, 110, 113, 123, 125, 128–129, 136–137; Walt Disney Productions, 96 (bottom); Wide World Photos, 42, 54–55, 76, 90, 96 (top), 108, 140–141, 146–147.
Cover: SPORTS ILLUSTRATED photograph by Heinz Kluetmeier © Time Inc.

Lyrics to "Yepremian's Lament," pp. 58–59: © Ted Lampidis.

Library of Congress Cataloging in Publication Data
Rubin, Bob. Little men of the NFL. (The Punt, pass, and kick library)
SUMMARY: Brief biographies emphasizing the careers of seven professional football stars who are of smaller and lighter build than the average player.
1. National Football League—Juvenile literature. 2. Football—Juvenile Literature. [1. National Football League. 2. Football—Biography] I. Title.
GV955.5.N35R82   1974   796.33′2′0922 [B]   [920] 74-5145
ISBN 0-394-82807-0   ISBN 0-394-92807-5 (lib. bdg.)

Manufactured in the United States of America   1 2 3 4 5 6 7 8 9 0

To Sam, Ali, Fang, Aps, Nat, Adele, Jackie,
Kitsky, Cleo, Honey, Bernie, Patricia,
Daniel, Peter, Elaine, Adam, Ben, Wilma . . .
and, above all, Penny

Contents

Introduction

A man who stands 6-feet tall and weighs 190 pounds would be considered a bruiser in most professions. Only in the National Football League could he be called little. But of course most professions are not peopled by the 6-foot-6, 260-pounders so common in the NFL.

Reduced to its essentials, football is a game of blocking and tackling. Reduced to their essentials, blocking and tackling simply mean knocking your opponent off his feet. The bigger and stronger a player is, the better equipped he is to put his man on his back—or prevent his opponent from flattening *him*. That's why football has always been and will probably remain a big man's game.

That is not to say there is no place in the game for smaller men, however. Far from it. Even in the land of the giants, good little men can—and do—have great success. They earn a place for themselves by

being just a little faster than their competition . . .
or a little smarter . . . or a little tougher . . . or
maybe just a lot more determined.

But no matter how determined he is, it's never
easy for a little man to succeed in the NFL's violent
world. Owners, general managers, and coaches all
admit they're biased in favor of the bigger player. So
in addition to the obvious physical difficulties he
must face, the little man in football must also
surmount an imposing psychological barrier—the
natural skepticism of the men he must impress to
win a job. In a game in which only the fittest survive,
the successful little man must often prove himself to
be the fittest of the fit.

In the following chapters, we shall meet seven
men who found a way to do just that—seven "little"
men who made a big mark in the National Football
League.

LITTLE MEN
OF THE NFL

1.

Fran Tarkenton

When the Minnesota Vikings faced the Green Bay Packers in 1964 it looked like a classic David and Goliath match-up.

Only in their third year of play, the Vikings were a typically ragged expansion team, a collection of inexperienced youngsters, aging veterans cast off from the more established teams, has-beens, and never-weres. The Packers, on the other hand, were charter members of the NFL who represented the very essence of the pro football establishment.

The ragtag Vikings had never beaten the powerful Packers. And now, with less than a minute to play, they seemed to be headed for still another loss. Trailing by two points, the Vikings faced a seemingly hopeless fourth-down-and-22 situation on their own 36-yard line. Knowing Minnesota had to try a pass,

In 1964 quarterback Fran Tarkenton leads the rag-tag Vikings to their first victory ever over the mighty Green Bay Packers.

the Packers spread seven defenders downfield, some as deep as 40 yards from the line of scrimmage.

The young Viking quarterback didn't even bother to call a play. All he said in the huddle was, "Everybody eligible to catch a pass get on your horse."

The quarterback was Fran Tarkenton, and he was about to put on a show.

Tarkenton did not drop back into the protective pocket formed by his blockers, the usual beginning of an NFL pass play. Instead, he began to scramble. He darted around the backfield hoping that if he could hang in there long enough, one of his receivers would somehow get free.

The huge Packer linemen took up the chase, cursing under their breath. They had played this cat-and-mouse game with the elusive little man known as "Fran the Scram" before. Tarkenton raced off to his right with Green Bay end Willie Davis in hot pursuit. Davis threw his 250 pounds at him, but the Viking quarterback scrambled out of harm's way.

"That little so-and-so took three years off my career," Davis said later. "He just plain wore me out."

Packer tackle Henry Jordan picked up where Davis left off. For a moment Jordan seemed to have Tarkenton trapped, but the lithe quarterback executed a graceful pirouette and the 260-pound Jordan was left clutching at the air.

Tarkenton started, stopped, darted, and dodged,

retreating all the way to his own 10-yard line before weaving back toward the line of scrimmage. Back and forth, up and down. Bodies were flying all over the field.

Finally, Tarkenton spotted Viking receiver Tom Hall all alone 30 yards downfield. The quarterback threw on the run, but as the ball sped toward Hall and a vital first down, Gordie Smith, another Viking pass catcher, wandered onto the scene. Smith leaped, grabbed the ball out of Hall's hands, landed, and fell out of bounds. First down. Then Fred Cox came in and kicked the field goal that gave the Minnesota Vikings their first victory ever over the mighty Green Bay Packers. Chalk one up for the Scrambler.

Francis Asbury Tarkenton did not look like a professional quarterback. The 185-pound 6-footer stood about three inches shorter and weighed about 20 pounds less than the minimum standards a college signal caller must meet even to be considered a pro prospect. Tarkenton himself admitted he couldn't throw a football nearly as far or as fast as most of his peers.

And then there was his scrambling, which ran completely counter to the accepted rules of quarterback behavior. Until Tarkenton came along, coaches taught their signal callers that the eleventh commandment read, "Thou shalt stay in the pocket." Fran's unorthodox style went against his coach's grain, but it was the opposing NFL defensive linemen who really found it hard to take.

In fact, Baltimore's All-Pro defensive end Gino Marchetti went so far as to predict that someday Tarkenton would get killed as the result of one of his scrambles. "The game was not invented by God to be played that way," rasped Marchetti. The 260-pound end slumped on the bench, his massive chest heaving after unsuccessfully chasing Tarkenton all over the field one hot autumn afternoon.

"It's the kid I'm thinking about," Marchetti continued. "He seems like a pretty good kid. Personally, I'm not a man to bear grudges. But there are defensive ends in this league who don't think they should be playing fox-and-hounds when the temperature is 85 degrees. The reason is that a lot of them are fat and out of shape, and something terrible could happen to Francis if they get mad someday."

Despite such dire warnings, Fran the Scram managed to enjoy remarkably good health throughout his long, distinguished career. Through the end of the 1973 season, his thirteenth as a professional, Tarkenton never missed a single game because of injury.

During that period Tarkenton threw 4,449 regular-season passes, completing 2,459 (55.2 percent) for 33,248 yards and 249 touchdowns. Altogether, his completion yardage totaled nearly 19 miles through the air! In all of pro football history, only Johnny Unitas and John Brodie (who had played five

Fran the Scram scrambles past a San Francisco defender.

and four years longer than Tarkenton) had thrown more times and completed more passes. But Fran the Scram was close behind and gaining fast.

Throwing wasn't Tarkenton's only weapon. The little scrambler was the only man in pro football history to average over six yards per rushing attempt for more than 500 carries. Neither Jim Brown, Gale Sayers, O. J. Simpson, Larry Csonka nor anyone else could match "that little so-and-so" run for run. And of course on every one of his jaunts, Tarkenton was taking the chance that those huffing and puffing 260-pounders would finally catch up to him and squash him like the bothersome little gnat they thought he was.

Named for Francis Asbury, the first Methodist bishop to come to America from England, Fran Tarkenton was born February 3, 1940, in Richmond, Virginia. He was the second of Reverend Dallas Tarkenton's three sons. Very early in life Fran began to display an unusually analytical interest in sports, especially football. When he was only six, he collected countless pictures of football players which he arranged in teams on the living room floor. Setting up imaginary games with them, he developed an interest in and ability to call plays.

Fran first put his football theories into practice three years later when his family moved to Washington, D.C. Fran then joined the Merrick Boys' Club, where he started off as an end on the twelve-and-under football team. He also played basketball, and in the spring of 1951 he was selected to the All-Washington twelve-and-under baseball team as a shortstop. He was terribly disappointed when his family moved to Athens, Georgia, just two days before the team was scheduled to play a televised game in Griffith Stadium, home of the then major league Washington Senators.

But Fran's disappointment didn't last long. By the fall of '51 he was quarterbacking the Athens YMCA team and had already forgotten Washington. Though he was still a relative stranger in town, the new boy quickly established himself as a leader. That winter he led the Athens Y to the state basketball championship. And that spring he pitched eleven straight victories, including three no-hitters, for an Athens Little League team.

Fran became a one-boy athletic department at Athens High. He pitched two more no-hitters for the baseball varsity, played shortstop when he wasn't on the mound, and was the team's leading hitter. In basketball he was the varsity's top scorer in both his junior and senior years. And as quarterback of the Athens football team, he completed 54.3 percent of his career passes. In his junior year he led the Trojans to a perfect 13–0 record and the state championship. Remarkably, he did not have a single pass intercepted that whole season. Experts called that 1955 Athens team one of the greatest in Georgia high school history.

The next year several Athens starters graduated

and Fran led the badly weakened team. One of their first games was against powerful Baylor Prep. "They were considerably out of our class," Athens coach Weyman Sellers admitted. "So we decided to put on a show. We had Francis pass almost every play we had the ball. He threw 52 times and completed more than half for over 200 yards. Baylor won easily, but we scored two touchdowns on Francis' passes—the only time Baylor's goal line was crossed that year."

Fran's outstanding play attracted the attention of college scouts all over the country, but he chose the University of Georgia, which was just a few blocks away from his home. Tarkenton led the freshman team to an undefeated season in 1957, then made a characteristically dramatic varsity debut the following year. Entering a game in which Georgia trailed Texas 7–0 in the third quarter, Fran immediately marched the Bulldogs 95 yards for a touchdown and then completed a pass for a two-point conversion and an 8–7 lead.

As a junior in 1959 Tarkenton set a Southeastern Conference record for passing accuracy by completing 62 of 102 attempts for a 60.8 percentage. One completion Georgians talked about for years afterward came on November 14 against Auburn, and it gave the Bulldogs the Southeast Conference championship and a bid to the Orange Bowl.

Auburn was leading 13–7 with just three minutes left to play when the Bulldogs recovered a fumble on Auburn's 35-yard line. Two passes failed, bring-

Tarkenton calls the signals in the Viking huddle.

ing up a crucial third-and-10. Tarkenton kept Georgia hopes alive by hitting end Don Soberdash for consecutive gains of 16 and 9 yards, advancing the ball to the Auburn 10.

Fran's next two passes lost two yards, and with just 30 seconds to play he was faced with a do-or-die fourth-and-3 call. Tarkenton flooded the right side of the field with receivers, faded, looked to his right, cocked his arm, and threw to end Bill Herron—who was standing all alone in the *left* corner of the end zone.

There were many more memorable Tarkenton

performances at Georgia . . . his two touchdown passes in the ensuing 14–0 Orange Bowl victory over Missouri . . . his six completions in seven attempts and a brilliant 19-yard scramble in the 1959 opener that sparked a 17–3 victory over Alabama, the powerful Tide's lone defeat all season . . . his 19 completions in 24 throws for 224 yards against Mississippi State in 1960 that almost single-handedly transformed a 17–7 Georgia deficit into a heart-stopping, last-minute 20–17 win.

As the Georgia team captain in his senior year, Tarkenton completed 58.4 percent of his 185 pass attempts, led the SEC in total offense with 1,274 yards, made the All-America Academic first team for his brilliant scholastic record, and won second team Associated Press All-America honors for his football prowess. In critical situations Tarkenton was even used in the Georgia *defensive* backfield, where he twice came up with key interceptions. Altogether he averaged 50 minutes of playing time per game.

The rest of the country got a chance to see Tarkenton in action when he was selected to play in the Hula Bowl in Hawaii after his final college season. Passed over as the East's starting quarterback by Notre Dame coach Joe Kuharich, Fran didn't get into the game until the middle of the second quarter. Making up for lost time, Tarkenton immediately marched the East 90 yards for a touchdown. Another long East drive in the fourth quarter ended with an eleven-yard touchdown pass.

The East won 14–7, and Tarkenton won the Governor's Cup and a host of national headlines for his 19 completions in 33 attempts for 204 yards.

The fans may have been impressed with Tarkenton, but the pro scouts apparently were not. "Too small, mediocre arm," read their reports. The Vikings, who were about to begin their first NFL season, finally picked Fran in the third round, hardly a vote of confidence for a quarterback with his credentials. But Tarkenton had enough confidence of his own. "Believe it or not," he said later, "the thought that I didn't have the stuff for the NFL never entered my mind. It is just not part of my philosophy to question myself or to think negatively. I always try to leave that sort of thinking to others."

Tarkenton became a pro in 1961, but he still had a lot to learn. For example, when Viking equipment manager Stubby Eason suggested Fran wear a double face bar on his helmet instead of the single bar he'd used all through college, the rookie said no thanks. But in Tarkenton's first exhibition game he learned how right Eason had been. Stopping for a split second to admire a pass he had just released, Tarkenton saw stars when Baltimore Colt tackle Billy Ray Smith smashed him across the bridge of his nose—right where the second bar would have been. "They poured me on the bench the way you'd pour a can of heavy oil," Tarkenton recalled with a rueful grin. "I was still lying there wondering what country I was in when Norm Van Brocklin [the Vikings'

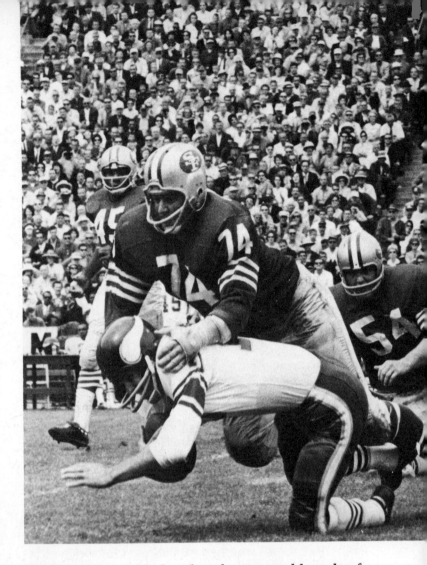

coach] came over and said in that inimitable style of his, 'Welcome to the National Football League, kid.'" From then on, Tarkenton wore a double bar.

It was Van Brocklin who taught Tarkenton another important lesson. Watching Fran loft high,

After a little too much scrambling, Tarkenton runs into trouble and is brought down by the 49ers.

soft, fat passes in practice, the coach explained in rather strong terms that in the NFL you either zip the ball or get zapped. To make sure Fran got the message, Van Brocklin had him lift a five-pound dumbbell 25 times a day to strengthen his throwing arm. He also made Fran carry an NFL football wherever he went in order to get the feel of the pro ball, which is slightly fatter around the middle than the one used in college. "That made me feel like the dumbest kid in kindergarten," Tarkenton said. "See the football. See how it's shaped. See how the laces run down the middle of the football. Now throw the football. See how it wobbles."

The Vikings' opponents continued the rookie's education. The Chicago Bears had a complicated, highly varied defense in those days, designed to confuse the enemy quarterback. They put it to good use in a 1961 exhibition against Minnesota and absolutely befuddled Francis Asbury Tarkenton. "I was demoralized, panicky, and totally unsure of how to handle this team of blitzing dervishes," said Tarkenton—the first and only time in his career he admitted to any self-doubt about his future as a pro.

The doubts lasted just one week, however. The following Sunday in another preseason game, Tarkenton led the Vikings to two quick touchdowns against the Los Angeles Rams and decided he could make it in the pros after all. His teammates, some of them grizzled veterans, began to agree with him.

On one play against the Rams, Hugh McElhenny, a superb but aging runner, broke loose for a 50-yard gain. McElhenny was somewhat winded when he returned to the huddle, so he asked Tarkenton not to use him on the next play. Tarkenton could have deferred to the veteran, but he knew that to succeed in the NFL, a quarterback must be the absolute ruler in the huddle.

Tarkenton called McElhenny's number again. The big running back glared at the nervy rookie but later told Van Brocklin, "When the kid called my play the second time, I knew we had a quarterback."

The Vikings opened the first regular season in their history against the same Chicago Bears who had given Tarkenton so much trouble in the preseason. This time Fran was ready, however, and he showed what a solid week of studying the Bears' defense on paper and on film could produce. Tarkenton completed 17 passes in 23 attempts for 250 yards and four touchdowns, ran for a fifth score, and was the chief engineer of the baby Vikings' 37–13 upset. "We were tied for first place in the National Football League and I had the game ball from my professional debut," Tarkenton said.

The rookie quarterback savored the rare moment —as well he might. The next time a Tarkenton-led team occupied first place was 13 years later. In between were seasons of great individual accomplishment, as evidenced by Fran's brilliant statistics and his selection to the Pro Bowl following the 1964, '65, and '66 seasons.

But none of that seemed to be helping the Vikings. They won only three of fourteen games in Tarkenton's rookie year, two in 1962, and five in 1963. Of course, without Tarkenton's 6,903 yards passing and 55 scoring completions, they might not have won any.

In 1964 the Tarkenton-led offense put more than 25 points per game on the scoreboard. More significant, the previously inept Viking defense finally did their part, holding opponents to an average of 21 (a full seven points better than their mark the season before). The Vikings finished that season with an 8–5–1 record, tying Green Bay for second place in the NFL's Western Conference and raising hopes that better days were ahead.

But those hopes were short-lived. Although Tarkenton threw for 2,609 yards in 1965, Minnesota's defensive improvement was only temporary. That year the Vikings gave up almost 29 points per game and the team fell back to fifth place. Yet when coach Van Brocklin erupted in angry frustration, his main target was his quarterback, of all people. Tarkenton became the team's scapegoat, and his scrambling style was blamed for all their woes.

Van Brocklin, one of the pocket passing stars of the 1950s, had reluctantly accepted Tarkenton's scrambling in the Vikings' first few seasons, recognizing a clear danger to Tarkenton's life and limbs if he had to depend solely on the Minnesota blocking crew. Masters of the "Look Out Block" (the would-be blocker yells "Look out!" as his man roars by him), the early Vikings formed a pocket that had more holes than Swiss cheese.

By the mid-60s, however, Van Brocklin thought the Viking offensive wall had improved enough for

Fran to stay where he belonged. Van Brocklin doubted that a scrambler could ever win a championship. He said that Tarkenton "would win some games he shouldn't but would also lose some he shouldn't."

Far more serious, he accused Tarkenton of being a selfish player, one who put his own statistics over his team's welfare. Enraged by the unfair charge, Tarkenton sent a letter to the Vikings' owners on February 9, 1967, demanding to be traded.

"I'd be the first to admit that there were times when I shouldn't have gone off on those wild scrambles," Fran said. "Van Brocklin's beef was that I could have gotten rid of the ball quicker, and a lot of times he was right. As the years went by, I worked on that. But he was wrong when he said I was doing it for selfish reasons. He gave people the idea I was trying to put on a show to make myself bigger box office and that I was sacrificing the good of the team. That was a bunch of bull."

On March 8, 1967, Tarkenton was traded to the Giants for four high draft choices. Ironically, Van Brocklin also left the Vikings in 1967 and his replacement, Bud Grant, quickly led the Vikings to four straight NFC Central championships. Four stalwarts of Grant's dynasty were running back Clint Jones, wide receiver Bob Grim, tackle Alan Page, and guard Ed White. All four were obtained by the Vikings with the Giant draft choices they got for Tarkenton.

Tarkenton, meanwhile, continued his streak of

Playing with the Giants in 1968, Fran gets set to pass while teammate Pete Case blocks out Washington's Carl Kammerer.

bad luck. He joined a Giant team deep in a slump after three straight NFL Eastern Conference championships in the early 1960s. Life in New York was depressingly familiar to Tarkenton. In his five years with the Giants the team finished 7–7, 7–7, 6–8, 9–5, and 4–10. Again Fran had some great individual seasons . . . 3,088 yards passing and 29 touchdowns in 1967 . . . 2,918 yards and 23 TDs in 1969 . . . Pro Bowl appearances every year except 1971. But as he had already learned, one man's accomplishments can never make up for the deficiencies of a basically weak team.

Fran's brilliant efforts could do no more than lift a poor team to mediocrity. Only in 1970 was there any break in New York's dismal records. That year the Giants held their opponents to 270 points and missed the playoffs by just one game. The following year, however, they gave up 362 points and dropped back to the bottom of the league. Tarkenton had been through it all before, including the subsequent booing from the home crowd and sniping from the press. It was Fran—not his team—they called "loser."

Once more, tension arose between Tarkenton and his coach. Once again, the coach (this time it was Alex Webster) wanted Tarkenton to curb his on-the-field improvisations even though neutral observers thought it was precisely those improvisations that were keeping the Giants from total defeat.

The last straw for Tarkenton came when the Giants began planning a massive rebuilding program for 1972. At 32, the last thing in the world Fran wanted was to be part of a rebuilding program. "I wouldn't mind playing for a strong team," he said. "I would love the chance to get into the Super Bowl before I retire, but I'm through with rebuilding programs. I'm tired of them."

Meanwhile, the Vikings were having troubles of their own. Joe Kapp, their quarterback during their championship reign, had left Minnesota after a salary dispute. The Vikings were in desperate need of a top-flight signal caller to go with a team that now appeared to have everything else. So in the summer of 1972 Tarkenton was traded back to Minnesota for wide receiver Bob Grim, quarterback Norm Snead, running back Vince Clements, and two high draft choices.

Tarkenton couldn't have been happier. In his absence the Vikings had built a powerful team, especially on defense. Nicknamed the "Purple People Eaters," the ferocious Viking defensive unit included All-Pro end Carl Eller, All-Pro tackle Alan Page (the first lineman ever named the NFL's Most Valuable Player), Gary Larsen and Jim Marshall. With that kind of support Tarkenton seemed sure to rid himself of the "loser" label and lead his team to the elusive championship.

"Going back to the Vikings has made me feel ten years younger," Fran exulted. "It's a great chance, a

Back with the Vikings in 1973, Fran meets and beats Green Bay again.

fortunate opportunity, a wonderful break. I am so excited about this coming season. I just can't remember being this anxious to get started."

By midseason, however, Fran couldn't wait for the year to end. Tarkenton was as good as ever, but injuries to Page and Eller badly handicapped the vaunted Viking defense. Playing the toughest schedule in the NFL that year, the Vikings lost four of their first five games by a total of eleven points.

Preseason Super Bowl favorites, the Vikings finished 7–7, their string of division titles snapped at four by Green Bay. The year before, Minnesota had alternated three nonentities at quarterback, yet won a championship. Now, with a Pro Bowl selection throwing for 2,651 yards and 18 touchdowns, they dropped to third. Of course the year before, the famed Purple People Eaters had given up only 139 points to opponents, less than ten per game. The year Tarkenton rejoined them, they yielded 252, or 18 per game.

After that 1972 season, Tarkenton talked about his twelfth straight unsuccessful quest for a championship. "I wanted to win," he said. "I wanted to win very much. But not any more than anybody else. The team expected to win. The team should win.

"If I can win a championship, it won't change me one way or the other. I want to win a championship. I want to win one desperately. It's probably what I want right now more than anything else in the world. But if I don't, I'm not going to kill myself.

And if I do win a championship, it will probably make me happier than anything else could—right now. But in a few years, it won't make much difference."

With their defensive big guns healthy again, Tarkenton finally led the Vikings to a championship in 1973 and shed the reputation that had plagued him for so long. Interestingly, Dallas, the team the Vikings beat in the NFC title game, was quarterbacked by Roger Staubach, whose nickname Roger the Dodger was a tribute to his ability to scramble.

The Vikings didn't quite go all the way, falling in the Super Bowl to a Miami Dolphin team considered among the greatest in pro football history. At quarterback for Miami? A cool young scrambler named Bob Griese. It seems that scramblers can be winners after all. Color, talent, coolness under fire, durability, and intelligence . . . Tarkenton had them all. Now after 1973 he also had a Super Bowl appearance. But there was still one thing he lacked —a Super Bowl victory to prove that all his talents (and a squad of skillful teammates) could add up to a championship.

2.

Floyd Little

Denver Bronco quarterback Steve Tensi barked signals in the crisp October air as the Houston Oiler defense jumped around trying to anticipate where the play would unfold. Suddenly the ball was snapped, and two lines of massive men collided with a crack as loud as a rifle shot.

Tensi whirled and handed off to a short, chunky, bowlegged back with number 44 emblazoned in brilliant orange across his uniform. Displaying instant acceleration, the trademark of all great runners, the little running back darted through a tiny hole opened by his blockers and shot into the Oilers' secondary.

One of the great moments of pro football was taking place. Floyd Little had the ball in an open field.

An Oiler linebacker dove at Little. Displaying another natural skill found in all great runners, the Bronco back spotted the defender out of the corner of his eye and skittered crablike out of reach, leaving the Oiler linebacker with nothing but a faceful of dirt.

Little roared upfield, the target of a converging mass of tacklers. He sped straight at one of them, faked with his head and shoulders, and left the man frozen on the spot.

Another tackler lunged at Little and got a tenuous hold on the 5-foot-10, 195-pound back—but not for long. Little spun in a full circle, ripped free and sped off in a different direction. Looking clumsy next to Little's balletlike turns and twists, the Houston defensive unit lumbered after him.

A fleet safety hurled himself in a flying cross body block in an attempt to knock the Bronco ball-carrier off his feet. Little was hit hard, but instead of going down, he simply bounced a few feet sideways and continued running. By this time there were bodies strewn all over the field as one by one the blockers and tacklers were knocked down or collapsed in exhaustion. But Floyd Little danced on.

Finally, a Houston defender grabbed him by one leg and held on. Floyd dragged him several yards before the rest of the posse arrived. Then the little Bronco and the big Oilers collapsed in one dusty heap. The play had gained a total of 35 yards, but to get it Little had zigzagged at least a hundred.

Then the booing began as the crowd saw the referee's yellow flag on the ground back upfield. Denver had been called for clipping, so the incredible play was nullified. Little shook his head in disgust. It was 1967, his rookie year in the National Football League, and nothing seemed to be going right.

After an outstanding career as an All-America at Syracuse University, Little had been Denver's top draft choice. But after paying a reported $130,000 to sign him, the Broncos were beginning to wonder if Little was worth it. Though he showed flashes of brilliance—like that run against Houston—Little's professional career did not start off well.

Part of the problem was the great physical and emotional adjustment all players must make when they move from college to pro ball. More significant was the fact that the Broncos were having troubles of their own when Little joined them. Perennial losers, the Broncos had finished last in the American Football League's Western Division in both 1965 and 1966. Naturally, they could not provide Little with the kind of blocking help essential to the success of any runner, nor could they pose enough other threats on offense to keep opposing defenses from concentrating solely on Little.

Bronco fans, however, refused to look at the situation logically. As they saw it, here was this hotshot All-America from the East getting all that money and not earning it. Called "a $130,000

Bronco running back Floyd Little gets a jersey tackle from Cincinnati linebacker Bill Bergey.

lemon," Little was booed for failures he was power-
less to prevent. It was a tough situation, but if
anyone in Denver expected Floyd Little to fold up,
quit, and slink back home, they were in for a
surprise. Floyd Little had faced far tougher obstacles
before, and he had overcome them all. Making good
in pro ball was just one more hurdle in a struggle he
had been waging against long odds since his childhood.

Floyd Little was born July 4, 1942, in Waterbury,
Connecticut. His father died of cancer when Floyd
was six, leaving Mrs. Little to raise six children on
meager welfare payments in a poor black section of
town.

Floyd was a homely, troubled child. For a long
time he was afraid to go out of the house unless he
could cling to an older sister's skirt. Other children
mocked him. He was so self-conscious that after
mispronouncing a word in the third grade and being
laughed at by his classmates, he refused to read
aloud in school for years.

Floyd even went through a period of hiding under
his bed when he became convinced that his family
hated him because his skin was a darker shade than
theirs.

"I just couldn't stand to mix socially," Little
admitted years later. "I stayed in the house, hid
under the bed, and watched television. I guess I
watched every TV program they ever put on the
screen. That's why the neighborhood kids gave me
the nickname, 'Television Kid.' "

Ptomaine poisoning forced Little to miss the fourth grade, then repeat it. When he regained his health, he immediately went to work to help support his family. "I just hustled," he said. "I sold papers, worked as a stockboy, and averaged around five dollars a day shining shoes."

When Floyd was in the seventh grade he started to play sandlot football. "I played in the line," he recalled. "I liked coming up to make the tackle. But I was still working after school, and I had to watch that I didn't ruin my clothes. So I wasn't too tough in those days."

When he was 13 his mother moved to a run-down neighborhood in New Haven, Connecticut. There were 26 children on three floors in one house in which the Littles lived. But by that time Floyd had found an interest in life that allowed him to forget the grinding poverty and hopelessness of ghetto life at least part of the time. He had discovered sports.

Floyd was one of the best halfbacks in the history of Hillhouse High School. But unfortunately, he was far from being one of the best students. So when his football eligibility ended after his junior year when he turned 19 (because of the year he'd missed way back in the fourth grade), Floyd had nothing. His grades weren't good enough to get him into college. "In school they had me on a program of shop and physical education," he recalled. "When I got through, I couldn't even read well."

Little tried to get a job as a custodian but wasn't hired because he read so poorly that he couldn't

Little relaxes on the sidelines while the Denver defense takes over.

even fill out the application form. "All I was trying to be was a custodian," he recalled, "and I couldn't even handle that. But I was smart enough to know that I wasn't failing to get the job because I was black. I was failing because I couldn't read. I walked out of there knowing I'd never get the job, but I also knew I was going to come back and make it."

Little was told he had an IQ of 85 and that he would never make it in college. "I was told I was too dumb," he said. "But you try going without eating for two days and see how well you do on tests."

Little was at a crossroads faced by many fine athletes from poor backgrounds. Some simply give up and return to the ghetto permanently. Others find a way to make their physical talents work for them and lift them out of the cycle of poverty and ignorance. With the help of his Hillhouse coach, Dan Casey, Little found a way out. Casey wrote a letter about Floyd to Notre Dame. The Irish football staff was so impressed with Little's potential that they suggested he attend a prep school—at their expense—to raise his marks to an acceptable college level.

So Little went to Bordentown Prep, a military school in New Jersey. It was a turning point in his life. There he gained confidence and maturity. "Before, I never wanted to leave home," he recalled, "but then at Bordentown it seemed I never got home at all. My family started calling me 'Big Shot.'"

At Bordentown, Little was put in charge of a platoon and elected captain of the football, basketball, and track teams. More important, his grades improved so much that 46 schools besides Notre Dame tried to enroll him.

Syracuse football coach Ben Schwartzwalder was especially eager to get Little. "There's a kid from New Haven I'd love to get," Schwartzwalder told a friend in January, 1963. "He's so smooth that when he walks in the snow he doesn't leave footprints. But I'm afraid we're going to lose him to Notre Dame."

Schwartzwalder wasn't about to give up without a fight, though. He came up with a plan that involved Ernie Davis, a brilliant Syracuse running star whose background was similar to Little's. Davis was the second in what became a string of Syracuse All-America runners (Jim Nance and Larry Csonka followed), all of whom wore jersey number 44. The legendary Jim Brown, who later collected most of pro football's all-time running records as a Cleveland Brown, had been the first. The coach thought Davis might convince Little to be the third man to wear number 44 at Syracuse.

"Ernie was always my idol," said Little. "A lot of people thought that Jim Brown influenced me into going to Syracuse. But Brown was of a different era. He didn't mean that much to me. When I visited Syracuse in late fall of '62 I saw films of Ernie. But when I met him I was even more impressed. It wasn't just his being an athlete. It was his whole character."

44

Floyd certainly wanted to go to Syracuse. But he had a strong sense of responsibility, and he had always believed that Notre Dame had financed his education at Bordentown. Therefore, he felt obligated to go there. Late that spring, however, the dean of students at Bordentown assured him that the academy itself had paid his expenses. "From that moment on," said Little, "I felt independent."

A few days later, Little recalled, "I was working out on a field near Bordentown. This kid comes up, drinking a Coke. He said, 'You hear about Ernie Davis? He died.' I thought the kid was making a terrible joke. I got mad. I was gonna hit him. My dad died of cancer when I was six, but I really had no knowledge of leukemia. I saw Ernie at Christmas and he was as healthy as I was. But the kid convinced me it was true. I sat down and got sick. Right then I knew I was going to Syracuse."

In his first year at Syracuse, Little led the freshman team in rushing, scoring, and pass receiving, averaging over eight yards per run. Then he broke Davis' varsity sophomore rushing record (686 yards) with 828 yards. He also led the Orangemen in pass receiving, punt and kickoff returns, and scoring. His total offensive production of 1,686 yards averaged out to 168 yards per game.

"But I didn't really have a good year," Little said. "I really didn't start coming until the seventh game, against Pitt. I started seeing my cuts, started seeing the blocking angles, got my moves. Before that, it all seemed too much to handle."

But soon it was Little who was too much to handle. He finished his Syracuse career with 2,704 yards rushing, nearly 5,000 in total offense, and 46 touchdowns.

But to describe Little's performance at Syracuse merely in terms of numbers is like describing the Empire State Building by just saying it's 1,250 feet high. Each has to be seen to be truly appreciated.

Take the five-touchdown effort Little dramatically turned in against the University of Kansas in his Syracuse home varsity debut. Gale Sayers, who later became one of pro football's all-time running greats with the Chicago Bears, was then a star at Kansas. Sayers received most of the pregame publicity. But it was Little the people were talking about when the game was over.

In the first quarter Little went around left end from the Kansas 19-yard line. He got a block at the line of scrimmage, faked to the outside, cut to the middle, brushed off a tackler, and flew to the end zone.

A few minutes later he was off again, this time for 55 yards. He started off tackle, then funneled up the middle, bouncing from defender to defender, across the goal line.

"I think if you ran the play back slowly," said Ted Dailey, the Syracuse defensive line coach, "you'd

Syracuse's All-America Floyd Little runs for a touchdown, breaking the school's all-time rushing record.

find about eleven Kansas players either had a hand on him or a chance to tackle him."

Syracuse got close to the goal again and Little scored from a yard out. Later he scored from the 3. Sayers was just another anonymous Jayhawk by the time Floyd scored his fifth touchdown, climaxing the most dramatic debut anyone had ever made in the Syracuse stadium. Scoring touchdown number five, Little went off tackle from the 15. Three steps beyond scrimmage he seemed to tilt to his right like an overburdened sailboat. He glided into a group of defenders. Off one, off another. Acceleration. End zone. Final score: Little and company 38, Kansas 8.

Later that season, Little made what some Syracuse fans still call, in hushed tones, "The Run."

It came against Oregon State. Wally Mahle, the Syracuse quarterback, took the snap, straightened up, and lobbed a pass about five yards over the middle to Little. Both sides of the Oregon State defense collapsed on Little as he cut down the center of the field. The run was restricted to a path no more than ten yards between the waves of tacklers. It looked like the wagon train boss running a Sioux gauntlet in a John Wayne western. The Beaver safeties appeared to close the gap at the 20-yard line. But then came that fantastic Little acceleration, and Floyd raced into the end zone.

The crowd sat in stunned silence. They realized they had seen a once-in-a-lifetime run. Afterward, someone asked Little about his ability to accelerate like a giant jet leaving the runway. "It's just a gift," he said. "I have three different speeds and premeditated moves. I like to get close to a defender, at arm's length, then make my cut at a 45-degree angle. I can do it at top speed. The idea is to try to lock into the defender's eyes to see if he'll flinch, then juke [fake] him. If you watch his eyes, you'll know if there's enough time to cut.

"Some are faster, but I can run as fast sideways as I can straight ahead, which few can. I can accelerate fast and shift speeds smoothly. I'm small, but that helps me to hide. I mean it. I'm hard to spot behind big linemen. Also it's hard to get down to my legs, which is the only place to bring me down. I'm strong, I have good balance, and I make good use of my arms, which I swing to break tackles. I run skittery, like a mouse eluding a cat. I can't explain my moves. I don't think any good runner can. I can't copy anyone. I don't know what I'm doing until I do it, then I can never repeat it. It's some kind of instinct. I look at me on films and say, 'Jeez, that guy made a helluva move. What was that?' "

In addition to perfecting his football skills, Floyd matured greatly as a person at Syracuse. He became a team leader and at least a respectable student. In his freshman year Little had met a coed from St. Alban's, New York, named Joyce Green. A part-time model and an honor student, Joyce was the daughter of two schoolteachers. She and Floyd began to date, and they were married when he graduated in 1967.

Floyd Little goes over the top to gain some yards in the pros as the Broncos face the Oakland Raiders.

Little was drafted by the Denver Broncos that year, much to his dismay. Joyce and Floyd had both grown up in the East—and that was where they had hoped to remain. "I wanted to stay in the East because all my friends and contacts were there," Floyd said.

But that wasn't the only thing bothering Floyd. The Broncos were one of the weakest teams in the league. When he heard that they had drafted him, Floyd said, "Holy Smokes, how can they do this to me? I'm liable to get killed with that club. . . .

"I figured maybe the New York Jets or somebody could make a deal for me. Finally it dawned on me that there wasn't going to be any deal. We made plans to go out and look at Denver, but our hearts weren't in it. Joyce and I figured Denver was some hick town in the Wild West where people lived hip deep in snow half the time. But then we went out and found it seldom snows. It's cold, but so are other places. It's a beautiful town where a black man is treated beautifully. I just fell in love with the place."

Unfortunately, it took a little longer for Denver to fall in love with Floyd Little. He had that unimpressive rookie season during which he gained only 381 yards and averaged less than three yards per run. For the third time in a row, Denver finished in last place, winning just three games and losing eleven in 1967. Floyd was as disappointed with himself as were the Bronco fans.

"I was never used to losing," he said. "I never lost

a game in high school or at prep school, and I think we lost a total of five at Syracuse. But you got to crawl before you can walk. Things could have been tougher. They always can be tougher."

Always a hard worker, Little put in an even greater effort in 1968. "Counting variations, we had a thousand plays," Little recalled. "It took me a while to learn them, and it was hard to get my timing right carrying only once in a series. Even at that, I could have made a lot more yardage improvising. But the coach was building a team and he insisted I run the plays as designed and hit the holes even when they weren't there. That was tough to take. I was used to getting ten yards a crack, and I had to learn that sometimes one is hard to get. But soon our young blockers began improving and I was averaging five a crack. Now I can see it was all worthwhile."

Little also had to make important psychological adjustments. "One of the things you learn as a pro is that the other guys are good, too, and they're gonna beat you on some plays," he explained. "You've got to just forget it and fight back on the next play. You've got to take the long view of the season. You have to psych yourself to do your best no matter what. That's what you're being paid for."

By the last half of his second season it all began to come together for Little, and he started to dazzle pro fans as he had the people who watched him in college.

"I remember one play in one game late in that 1968 season," he said. "It wasn't the length of the run, which was short, or the game, which was just another game, but it was the execution of the play. It was perfect. Looking back on it, I seem to see it in slow motion. All the blocks worked. The hole was there. I hit it just right. Just like on the blackboard. All of a sudden, all the pieces of our jigsaw puzzle were falling into place."

His teammates were quick to spot the changes in Little. Quarterback Steve Tensi pointed out, "Floyd seemed all uptight for a season or so. He seemed alone and tense. He just started to loosen up late that season and then he was really rolling." Defensive captain Dave Costa commented, "Floyd's teammates when he broke in were as green as he was, so he had no one to turn to for help. New players are afraid to bug the coaches. So he just had to find his own way through a lot of tough games."

Floyd himself recognized his new maturity and understanding of pro football. He said, "Coach Saban used to scream and holler at me. I wasn't used to it and I didn't like it and I didn't like him. But now I can see that I wasn't a complete player, and he only screamed at those he thought had a chance. I'm small and I had to learn how to block, for example. They told me to hit my man before he hit me, to stick my head into his numbers and bring my helmet up into his jaw. I tried it against Ernie Ladd [a 6-foot-9, 320-pound tackle for the Kansas City

Little avoids the tackle of New York's Steve O'Neal in a 1969 game.

Chiefs] and couldn't reach his jaw. I had to learn technique."

Little didn't need any lessons in toughness, however. "Every time I carry the ball, I run as if it's the last time," he said. "To keep going in this game, you've got to make a distinction between pain and injury. I wouldn't play more than one game—the first one—if I let pain keep me out. Hell, every time I run off tackle I may get a minor concussion. But if I can still remember the plays, I'm going to stay in there.

"You can't tiptoe through games. If you're cautious you're through. You go all out and hope for the best. It's got to hurt when guys 220, 250, or 280 pounds land on you. You just look to be lucky."

But Little had more than luck going for him. Although the Broncos did not show a corresponding rise in the standings, Little's yardage totals shot up dramatically as he became adjusted to pro ball. From 1968 to 1973 his yardage totals were 584, 729, 901, a league-leading 1,333, 859, and 979.

A running back lives or dies on the condition of his legs. Fortunately for Little, his legs were extremely bowed. "Tacklers can't get their arms all way around them," he said. "I'm the most bow-legged runner who ever played the game. If you pushed my legs together, I'd be six-foot-two and a great wide receiver! Some guy comes along and gives me a pop on the side of the leg and my knee just straightens up into a normal position instead of getting all ripped up."

Little laughed as he described his legs, delighted at the laugh he got in return from his listener. Many superstars reach a point where they become irritated by all the attention they get from reporters and fans, but Little always seemed to enjoy it.

Floyd had a special feeling for children perhaps because he remembers his own unhappy boyhood. He spent several offseasons working with youth groups in Denver. Then in 1973 he took on an additional responsibility. Explaining that he would someday like to be a judge, the boy who once lost a janitor's job because he couldn't read the application form entered law school. "I do not choose to be a common man," Little once said. "It is my right to be uncommon . . . if I can."

Those who knew him well were already calling him Your Honor.

3.

Garo Yepremian

". . . *The game is ending and I hear him calling.*
He says, 'Garo, get ready to go in.
We need three points now and the game is over
And your kick will assure us of this win.'
Here comes the call,
My leg is ready and I rip into the ball.
I lift my head,
To find the football rolling back to me instead.
It's clear to me,
There'll be no three.
I've got the ball, I'll go for all.
Someone's in the clear,
I'll throw it there.
Oh God! My hand was too small.
I'll never know what made me throw,

I feel so low, I wanna hide.
The game's too long, I have done wrong,
They're laughing on the other side.
It is not wise at this time to return to the bench.
Too many big boys around with their fists in a
clench.
I'll have to find a good place to dig a trench.
I must kneel and I must pray,
For a win to end this day."

The song's title is "Yepremian's Lament," and it describes one of the strangest and funniest episodes in the history of professional football.

The time: January 14, 1973. The place: mammoth Memorial Coliseum in Los Angeles, site of Super Bowl VII. A crowd of 86,000 fans had gathered to see if the Miami Dolphins could beat the Washington Redskins and become the first team in NFL history to complete an entire season undefeated.

For three quarters it was a dull game. The Dolphins scored one touchdown in the first quarter and another in the second. Meanwhile, their defense was so effective that the Redskins penetrated Miami's territory just once in the entire first half.

With only 7:07 left in the game the Dolphins still led 14–0. Then they got ready to try a 43-yard field goal that would virtually clinch their 17th consecutive victory of the season and give them football's biggest prize. In came Miami's outstanding placekicker, Garo Yepremian, a bald, 5-foot-7, 160-pound former soccer player of Armenian ancestry.

No one expected high drama as the two teams lined up. The ball was snapped, Yepremian moved forward and kicked it.

Then the fun began.

The kick was low, and it hit one of the Miami linemen who was trying to block in front of Yepremian. When the ball bounced loose, Yepremian scooped it up and began to run. He should have just fallen down on it, but panicking at the wall of Redskins closing in on him, he attempted to throw the ball as far downfield as possible.

His arm went back, then came forward in a classic passing motion—but the ball did not. It squirted out of Yepremian's hand straight up in the air. Redskin defensive back Mike Bass looked at the football as it floated into his arms like a belated Christmas gift, then streaked down the sidelines before someone tried to make him give it back. The last Dolphin with a chance to stop Bass was Yepremian, but the little kicker was easily blocked out of the play.

Although they were still a touchdown behind with only a few minutes to play, Redskins on the sidelines were all but falling down from laughter as Bass streaked across the goal line for a touchdown. But Yepremian wasn't smiling as he faced what felt like a 1,000-mile walk back to the Miami bench.

"When it happened," Garo recalled, "I didn't want to come off the field on the Dolphin side. I wanted to go in the opposite direction. I didn't know

Garo's Goof: In Super Bowl VII, Yepremian's field-goal attempt bounces off his teammate's helmet (above). The loose ball was picked up by Garo, who tried to pass (below) with disastrous results.

what was going to be said to me on the bench. It's funny, coach [Don] Shula never did yell at me. When I first came off, he just said, 'You should have fallen on the ball.' He didn't ask me why I threw it. He didn't yell at me. He just said I should have fallen on it. I really expected more criticism than that.

"I know I can pass better than that. The first thing that went wrong is that I have small hands. Second, I didn't have the ball by the laces. Third, somebody touched my left hand when I was getting set to throw with my right.

"I didn't take time to get set. I thought I had a chance to turn a disaster into something good. I thought if I had just taken the ball and fallen down, people would have said I was a born loser. I wanted to do something positive, not just fall on it. I learned different. No, no, a thousand times no. I will fall on the ball. I was wrong. The coach was right."

Thousands of Dolphin fans in the Coliseum and watching on television observed the play in stunned disbelief. Krikor Yepremian, Garo's brother, was in the stands. He felt sick. "As soon as the kick was blocked I knew Washington was going to score, I don't know why," Krikor said. "When Garo started running with the ball I thought he might score a touchdown, and then, calamity.

"I sweated like I have never sweated before, from top to bottom. I didn't know what to expect. There was still time; anything could have happened."

Fortunately, the Dolphins hung on to win 14–7, and both Yepremians breathed a sigh of relief. But Garo worried about the kind of greeting he would receive when he returned to Miami. The night after the game he drove up to his Miami home, still depressed, still uncertain whether he should have hopped a quick plane back to Cyprus, the island in the Mediterranean where he was raised.

"It was quiet in the neighborhood when we were driving up," Garo recalled, "but when we got to our house, there were a hundred people waiting for us. They had posters stuck to the house and they threw rice and popcorn at my wife and I. That made me feel a lot better."

Garo felt better still when he received a letter that read:

I'm sure you're going to get a lot of kidding about what happened. I want you to know I am proud of what you have done in your three years in Miami. Some great things have happened to you and the team and now is the time to relax and enjoy it.

Don Shula.

Suddenly, the disaster didn't seem like such a disaster at all. Yepremian learned that Dolphin fans were not only forgiving, but they actually thought his momentous blunder was funny. He received some 300 letters after the Super Bowl, but only two could possibly be described as critical.

One fan in Fort Lauderdale suggested it was all the fault of substitute quarterback Earl Morrall, who held the ball on the ill-fated field-goal attempt. He wrote that Morrall should have picked up Garo and the ball and thrown them both downfield to fullback Larry Csonka for a first down.

The other harsh words came from a fan who was upset because Garo appeared on the postgame television interview bare-chested.

"Hey, I didn't know they were going to pull me in front of the cameras when they did," Garo said. "If I had known, at least I would have put on one of my ties. Even without a shirt."

The Yepremian brothers had a business designing ties. After the Super Bowl their sales volume increased 50 percent and they opened a fourth store in St. Petersburg to go with two in Miami and one in Fort Lauderdale. Quickly realizing there might be gold in Garo's goof, they made a tie featuring a little embroidered arm, a tribute to the littlest Dolphin's passing prowess.

A poster displaying the classic Yepremian passing form became another big seller. A month after the Super Bowl a "Garo Yepremian for Quarterback Club" opened in the Miami area, and thousands of members enrolled within just one week.

The song "Yepremian's Lament" was put out by

At 5-foot-8 and 150 pounds, Garo looks even smaller than usual as he poses with Charley Bradshaw, a 6-foot-6, 260-pound tackle.

Garo Enterprises, Inc., sold in the Garo Yepremian Shop, and sung by Garo. (On the flip side Garo sang something called, "How to Tell You.")

Yepremian also hit the banquet circuit usually reserved for more orthodox sports heroes. "People seemed afraid to ask me about it," Garo said, "but I would relieve their minds right away. I'd announce that I didn't come to tell them about my kicking, but about my passing.

"I would explain that a kicker doesn't get too much activity, anyway, and I wasn't getting any at all in the Super Bowl until the last couple of minutes. I got so bored I was checking around the Coliseum to see who was wearing my ties. I could tell that the people were getting bored, too. So I decided to do something to get them excited."

The people laughed and Yepremian laughed along with them. Perhaps never in sports history had a mistake been so celebrated—or so profitable. As Krikor put it, "Garo's the kind that can make comedy out of tragedy."

It was really another way of saying that Garo is resourceful, able to seize upon what appears to be a problem and turn it into an advantage. That's a trait shared by all the Yepremians, who had to take advantage of every opportunity to successfully escape from their war-torn birthplace.

Garabed Sarkis Yepremian was born on Cyprus on June 2, 1944. There he first began to develop the strength in his left leg that would someday make him a star in a new land thousands of miles across the Atlantic Ocean. "When I was four years old my father bought me a soccer ball," Garo recalled. "I kicked it always. We had a cement wall for practicing tennis near our house, and I made as much noise as I could kicking the ball against that wall."

Garo went to a missionary school run by Americans in his hometown of Lanarca. By the time he was 13, he was an outstanding soccer player and was the captain of his school team. But then civil war interrupted both his studies and his soccer.

The 500,000 Greeks who lived on Cyprus (an island smaller than Connecticut) and the 100,000 resident Turks began shooting at each other. "Many innocent people were dying by accident," Yepremian recalled. "The streets were unsafe. My father was a fabrics merchant, but the shooting made it difficult for him to carry on."

In 1960 the Yepremian family decided to emigrate to London. Determined to succeed, and fortified by an education that included facility in English, Greek, Armenian, and Turkish, Garo worked his way up to floor manager of a clothing firm before he turned 21.

Krikor, who also knew how to seize upon a promising opportunity when he saw one, had read about former Hungarian soccer player Pete Gogolak's breakthrough in American football and the flood of other European kickers that had followed him. Convinced that Garo's powerful left leg could

get him a college scholarship, he urged his brother to seek fame and fortune in America. In 1966, just one week before he was supposed to try out for London's famous Arsenal pro soccer team, Garo agreed to move to the United States with Krikor.

The Yepremians emigrated to Detroit, but Garo's lack of a high school diploma ruled out a college scholarship. Undaunted, Krikor went straight to the pros, getting Garo a successful tryout with the Detroit Lions.

Surviving an early teeth-rattling collision with Green Bay's ferocious middle linebacker Ray Nitschke ("I had kicked off and didn't understand why he was trying to hit me so hard," Garo said), Yepremian kicked 13 field goals in 22 attempts for the Lions in 1966 and made all 11 of his extra-point tries. In a 32–31 victory over the Minnesota Vikings the little Lion set an NFL record by booting six three-pointers.

But his success with the Lions proved short-lived. Head coach Harry Gilmer was fired after the 1966 season ended, and Joe Schmidt took his place. Schmidt continued to use Yepremian on extra points in 1967, but alternated him with Wayne Walker on field goals. Garo tried only six three-pointers and made two. In 1968 Schmidt put him on the taxi squad—a small group of players who practice with the team all week but do not suit up for the games

Playing with the Lions, Garo demonstrates his soccer-style kick.

on Sunday unless one of the regulars is injured. The only kicking Yepremian did was for Michigan in the minor Continental League, where he made six of ten field-goal tries. Walker and rookie Jerry DePoyster did the Lions' kicking.

After spending another season on the taxi squad, Yepremian was released by the Lions at the end of 1969. Many players would have been bitter about that kind of treatment, but Garo wasn't. His sunny disposition never changed. "Maybe it's because I'm a Gemini and I keep problems to myself, except when I'm home with my family," he explained. "When I'm outside, I want to be happy with my friends, not burden them with problems. Maybe it also has something to do with my Armenian ancestry. We were always in the middle of other countries—Iraq, Turkey, Russia. Whenever there were wars between Europe and Asia, the armies came through Armenia.

"There was a lot of suffering, but the people learned to make the best of it. Armenians believe if you smile and think pleasant thoughts about others, you'll also be happy. It works."

Out of football after his release by the Lions, Garo tried to get work on the assembly line of the Ford Motor Company and was turned down. He made ties in the basement of the Yepremian house, but they didn't sell. Life was grim, but not for long.

The Miami Dolphins were desperate for a field-goal kicker as the 1970 training camp period approached. Gene Mingo, Booth Lustig, Jim Keyes, and Karl Kremser all had tried and failed as Dolphin kickers. Based on a letter of recommendation from the Lions to Miami coach and general manager Don Shula, the Dolphins invited Yepremian to come on down for a tryout.

For a while he and Kremser dueled for the regular kicking job. Garo took over in the second game of the regular season, kicking two field goals in a 20–10 victory over Houston in the Astrodome, then cemented his claim on the position by booting two more in his Miami home debut—one of 40 yards and one of 47 yards drilled through a driving rain just before half time—to help the Dolphins upset the powerful Oakland Raiders, 20–13.

Yepremian went on to make all 31 of his extra-point tries and, far more important, led pro football in field-goal accuracy by booting 22 in 29 attempts. To top it all off, he made 11 of 15 from between the 40 and 49 yard lines. Thus he made the Dolphins a threat to score every time they crossed midfield. With Yepremian's help, the Dolphins climbed from a last-place 3–10–1 record to a 10–4 mark and their first playoff berth ever in 1970. Although Oakland eliminated Miami 21–14 in the opening round, the Dolphins were clearly on the rise.

In 1971 Miami turned in a 10–3–1 record. Yepremian had an even greater season, kicking 28 field goals in 40 attempts and making good on all 33 extra-point tries to lead the NFL in scoring with 117

Garo kicks a field goal for Miami despite the efforts of Cedrick
Hardman, the San Francisco 49ers' 6-foot-4 defensive end.

points. Included were seven of twelve three-pointers from beyond 40 yards.

The Dolphins met Kansas City in the opening round of the '71 playoffs. The two teams battled fiercely for four quarters, finishing in a 24–24 tie when the final gun went off. Because there had to be a winner and a loser, the two clubs went into sudden-death overtime. The first team to score would win the game—and a chance for the championship.

Incredibly, the teams played an entire fifth quarter and part of a sixth before the tie was finally broken. With 7:40 gone in the second overtime period, Yepremian calmly booted a 37-yard field goal straight through the uprights to give the Dolphins the first division championship in their brief six-year history.

Then it was on to the AFC championship game, where the Dolphins defeated Baltimore 21–0. The Dallas Cowboys finally ended Miami's dreams with a 24–3 Super Bowl triumph, but it was obvious that the powerful young Dolphins would be a force to reckon with in the future.

The Dolphins couldn't wait to start the 1972 season. Yepremian, sporting a new mustache that curled across his cheeks and ran into his sideburns, seemed to be more serious than usual as he practiced his kicking in the Dolphins' training camp. At least that's the way he struck reporters who were used to seeing a constant smile plastered across his expressive face.

Garo had an explanation for the apparent change. "The thing that might make you think that I'm more serious is my mustache," he said. "It covers most of my face, and when I'm smiling it doesn't show.

"I haven't changed," Garo continued. "I'm crazier this year than last year. But when you're out there kicking by yourself there is nothing you can think of which is humorous. It's not that I'm not as funny—I haven't been interviewed as often as I usually have. Garo is old material. When you're new in camp, everybody wants to talk to you. Especially when you're short and bald-headed. Now, after two years, they know more about me than I know myself."

Doug Swift, Garo's roommate, was eavesdropping on all of this. "What you need is a new scriptwriter," Swift joked. "Now, I could put together a package . . ."

Six months later Yepremian threw the first and last pass of his career in Super Bowl VII. No scriptwriter in the world could have dreamed up a more spectacular attention-getter than that.

Of course, Garo had done his part in getting the undefeated Dolphins to the Super Bowl in the first place. In 1972 he made 24 of 37 field-goal tries and 43 of 45 extra-point attempts during the regular season to finish with 115 points, fourth best in the NFL. Three of his field goals were 50 yards or more, the most kicked of that length by anyone in pro football.

With three outstanding seasons behind him, Garo Yepremian was a long way from the soccer fields of Cyprus. Considering his own background, it was surprising to learn he felt it was wiser for pro teams to scout American campuses for young soccer-style kicking talent, rather than look to Europe.

According to Garo, "Even if they find someone over there who impresses them in a tryout, it's no guarantee he'll be able to make the adjustment to kick an American football consistently well under pressure. The best way to do it is look for the kids who play soccer in this country and have some understanding of American football, too. The money would be better spent developing kickers here."

One young kicker Yepremian wouldn't mind seeing get lots of money was a 1973 All-City, All-County, and second-team All-State selection from a Miami high school. His name: Berj Yepremian.

"He would have been first-team All-State probably, but he's only 17 and he has another year to play," Garo said with brotherly pride. "When I brag about Berj, people say, 'Hey, you're talking about a kid who might take away your job someday.' I tell them, 'Hey, if somebody is going to take my place, I'd want him to be my own kid brother.'"

Judging by his own 1973 performance, the elder Yepremian wasn't ready to give up his job to anybody. Garo booted 25 field goals in 37 attempts, nine of 40 yards or more. That made him an almost

unanimous choice of the experts as the NFL's All-Pro kicker. And Miami swept to another AFC East championship that year. After playoff victories over Cincinnati and Oakland, Garo and the Dolphins prepared to meet the Minnesota Vikings for Super Bowl VIII.

Facing innumerable questions from the press about his last Super Bowl goof with his usual good humor, Yepremian said, "I think Don Shula plans to put the boxing gloves on me for this Super Bowl because my bare hands are lethal."

But there was no need for "Yepremian's Lament" this time. Garo contributed a 28-yard field goal and three extra points to the Dolphin effort—and he kept his hands to himself. The Dolphins' easy 24–7 victory made them only the second team in history to claim two consecutive Super Bowl championships and made many fans and experts think that Miami just might be the greatest team in the history of pro football.

Sitting in the stands, brother Krikor breathed a sigh of relief.

Yepremian gets off one of the two three-pointers he contributed to the Dolphins' 34–16 win over the Bengals in the 1973 AFC playoffs.

4.

Nemiah Wilson

The sun still retained its summer warmth, but the calendar said it was fall. So the boys who lived near McKinley High School in Baton Rouge, Louisiana, dropped their bats and baseballs and began to choose up sides for football.

In the late afternoon, while there was still enough light, dozens of boys gathered to play on the grassy lawn in front of the school one September day in 1958. Some were members of the high school team; others were not. A group of McKinley coaches stood at the sidelines, intently watching the game. They were scouting to see if there were any good prospects they had missed.

One small, slender McKinley sophomore who was not a member of the high school team greatly impressed the coaches with his speed, his moves and his obvious natural ability. They watched him take the ball and dart past the other players, some of whom were among the varsity's best. They decided they wanted him to play for McKinley. But much to their surprise, Nemiah Wilson didn't want to join the team.

"It's fun to play when you want to play, not when someone says you have to play," Nemiah explained. "Nobody tells you, 'Do this or do that,' or makes you practice at a certain time."

But the McKinley coaches didn't give up. Instead they went to see Nemiah's mother. The Wilsons—Nemiah, his mother, and his four sisters and two brothers—lived in a poor black section of the city. Mrs. Wilson had been separated from her husband since Nemiah was a baby, and to support her family she worked at two different jobs. All the children helped out as much as they could. Nemiah, for instance, sold papers, mowed grass, caddied, and worked as a delivery boy. "Everyone pitched in as soon as they came of age," he explained.

So when the coaches told Mrs. Wilson that football might eventually provide a way for Nemiah to get a college education, she said she would speak to her son. It was a unique switch. Usually, it's the boy who has to convince his mother to let him play football.

Smiling at the memory, Nemiah recalled, "When I got home that night, my mother said she wanted to talk to me. She said she wanted me to play because my older brother Charles had always wanted to but was too small, which was true. Finally, she insisted that I play, so I did."

Just 5-foot-7 and 115 pounds, Nemiah was very small for football. Neither he, nor his mother, nor even the coaches ever imagined what a long, up-and-down road Nemiah had embarked upon when he agreed to play.

For although football did eventually provide a different way of life for him, giving him the opportunity to go to college and later earn a handsome living as a professional star, it also brought frustration and heartache to Nemiah Wilson.

Years later, as a fully grown 6-footer, weighing 165 pounds, Wilson was still considered "small." He never felt truly accepted in the big man's game.

"I've always had to fight to prove I belong," he explained. "I don't think I've ever had peace of mind no matter what kind of job I've done. A little man is always tagged. There's always a feeling that people are thinking you have no business being out there, that you're nothing but scrimmage bait. My whole idea has always been that if you can do the job then you should be accepted. But after you do the job and people still look at you as if they're wondering what you're doing out there, you start to

Nemiah Wilson (26) of the Oakland Raiders brings down the Buffalo Bills' big man, O. J. Simpson.

wonder what else you have to do. It's a fight that I really don't think I can ever win."

There's no question that Nemiah Wilson did his job well. He became a star at McKinley High, a star at Grambling, where he went to college, and a star in the National Football League, first with the Denver Broncos and then with the Oakland Raiders. Nevertheless, at every level of football he played, people looked first at his physical size rather than the size of his talent, and they simply couldn't believe he was really a football player.

Wilson's battle for acceptance began back in Baton Rouge almost the minute he agreed to play on his high school team. He began as a sophomore defensive back whose job was to intercept or knock down passes. But he had trouble showing the coaches what he could do because they wouldn't let him play with the first team for fear he would get hurt.

As a junior he was shifted to running back and finally made the first team. But even then he was only allowed to run with the ball against McKinley's weakest opponents. The rest of the time he would just carry out fakes while someone else ran. "They were still protecting me," he explained. "It hurt me a lot."

The McKinley team wound up winning the Baton Rouge championship that year. They were playing for the state title when their star runner suffered a pulled muscle and several other injuries. Nemiah felt sure he would finally get an opportunity to prove himself against top competition, but the coaches started the injured star anyway. "He ran all the plays and I just faked," Wilson recalled. "They just didn't figure I could do the job.

"The following year the star graduated and they didn't have anyone else but me. I scored 21 touchdowns in ten games, gained over 1,000 yards, and got a scholarship to Grambling. I had to fight to prove I was a football player, and eventually I did. That's the story of my life."

Actually, that was just the beginning. Round two of Nemiah Wilson's fight occurred at Grambling, a predominantly black school noted for its consistently powerful football teams and its large number of graduates who move on to professional teams. But when Wilson began college, the world of pro football seemed far out of reach.

"I had a defeatist attitude that I could never make it as a pro ballplayer, so I went there with the idea of concentrating on my education. I felt that if they thought that I was too small in high school, they would in college and so on down the line.

"When I got to Grambling they had All-Americas there who were just sophomores and juniors. I was number twenty-four on the list of running backs. I was back in the same bag. Grambling had big players, and when they saw me, the coaches wouldn't let me play. In my freshman year we played Texas College and we were beating them

30–0, or something like that, when they decided to let the rookies play. I ran the ball four times and scored three times, and I said, 'Well, now I'll get a chance to play.' I didn't. I mean you've got a school that carries twenty-four running backs and they're all good, so what do you do? What they did was play them according to seniority. Therefore, I was at the bottom of the list.

"I didn't get to play until my senior year when they switched me to the defensive backfield. I was a low sub as a sophomore and junior running back. Pro ball was the furthest thing from my mind. I could see the handwriting on the wall. By not playing, I knew I had no chance of being drafted, so I figured I'd better go ahead and prepare myself to do something with my education. I prepared myself to go out and teach."

And he well might have become a teacher if it hadn't been for a Grambling assistant coach named Oree Banks. When Wilson was ignored in the pro draft, Banks contacted friends of his on the Denver Broncos and told them that he knew a defensive back who might have pro potential. With nothing to lose but the $500 they offered Wilson to come to camp, the Broncos invited him for a tryout.

But Nemiah's past football frustrations made him hesitate to even accept Denver's offer. "I didn't go to Denver thinking too much of my chances," he said. "The only thing that made me go at all was my roommate. He said that any young guy who has an opportunity to try out for a pro team should go.

Wilson chases New England's Ron Sellers with no success, and the Patriot goes all the way for a touchdown.

Everyone else had told me all my life that I couldn't do it, that I was too small for pro ball, so I wasn't prepared to go. I said to myself, 'Why go and get hurt all over again?' But my roommate said, 'Hell, why not go just for the experience? You can always look back and say you were there.' I was curious so I went."

Wilson didn't have to wait long before he was reminded once again that he was a small man in a big man's game. It happened at the first Bronco team meeting in the summer of 1965. "Everybody was getting up and telling their height and weight," Wilson recalled. "One would get up and say, 'My name is Bob Smith, 6-foot-5 and 270,' and so forth. Then it got down to a couple of defensive backs in front of me and it was 6-foot-1, 205; 6-foot-2, 210. When it got to me I had to get up and say, 6 feet and 165 pounds. Everybody stopped and stared."

Wilson had seen those stares before—in high school and at Grambling—so once again he set out to prove that he was indeed a football player. And he knew there was only one way to do that. "I would have to prove myself against the best," he said.

The best in the 1965 Bronco camp was veteran Denver pass catcher Lionel Taylor, who four years earlier had caught 100 passes in one season, second most in pro football history. "They put me over on the same side of the field with Taylor because Willie Brown was the defensive back on the other side of the field," Nemiah recalled. "He was an all-league performer and no one competes with an all-league performer. All the other guys were afraid to try to cover Taylor because he had moves and hands, and they were afraid to look bad. I just figured that he was a normal man, so I tried him. The first couple of days I didn't know if I was coming or going. He was turning me inside out. But after about the third day I began to adjust to his moves and his way of thinking and I was able to stay with him. I would play him tight so he wouldn't have room to make his moves and throw me off. After the first couple of weeks I could handle him pretty well, and that's when the coaches began to think I might make the ballclub."

Wilson did make the team and became a starting cornerback, playing for the last-place Broncos in 1965, 66, and 67. As a cornerback, his main responsibilities were to defend against the league's fleet wide receivers on pass plays and to rush up from his position in the secondary to help stop sweeps around end when the enemy offense tried a run. In addition to his fine play at cornerback, Wilson returned kickoffs and punts, breaking loose for a 100-yard touchdown run on one kickoff. He also intercepted eight passes in those three seasons, running one of them back 70 yards for another touchdown.

Despite his small size, Wilson was quickly becoming a big success in the world's toughest league. Early in 1966 he dramatically demonstrated that he was more than strong enough to handle the giant backs and receivers who challenge a cornerback. In a game against the Houston Oilers he rushed up to stop Houston's bruising 235-pound fullback Hoyle Granger on two successive plays, meeting him in brutal head-on collisions and dropping him in his tracks both times.

Nevertheless, Wilson made it clear that if he'd had a choice, he would have used finesse rather than brute force to bring Granger down. "The physical part of the game has never really turned me on," he explained. "The mental part of the game has always been a challenge to me. That's what I like most. I feel you're just as effective if you can outmaneuver a guy as if you overpower him. If I can get the job done without the physical aspect, I'll do it. But if being physical is the only way, then I'll do that, too."

So Nemiah Wilson went on doing whatever had to be done. He did an outstanding job for a team that finished in last place three years in a row. At the end of the 1967 season Wilson was named to the American Football League's All-Star team, proof positive that he was considered one of the game's best players by his peers.

Unfortunately, the Denver management didn't quite share their enthusiasm for Wilson. After a salary dispute with the Broncos, Nemiah was traded to the New York Jets for a draft choice on July 10, 1968. But Nemiah wasn't able to agree to terms with the Jets either, and they released him in August.

Nemiah went home and just sat for three months, wondering if at the age of 25 he was through with football—or, more accurately, if football was through with him. He needn't have worried. In November the Oakland Raiders asked if he was interested in playing for them. He certainly was, and later that month he signed a contract that was even better than the one he had hoped for.

It was past midseason when Wilson joined Oakland, and the team was already involved in a red-hot race with the Kansas City Chiefs for the AFL's Western Division championship. The Raiders couldn't afford to let their newcomer learn while playing for fear of the mistakes he was bound to make in the process. So Wilson just sat on the bench for the rest of the '68 season and watched his new teammates capture their division crown before losing the league championship to the New York Jets.

Wilson was back in action the next year, however. Given a full six-week training camp period to learn the Oakland system, Nemiah became an immediate starter for the Raiders. After his three last-place seasons with the Broncos, Wilson now found himself in the thick of a tight championship race. The Raiders finished first in the AFL's Western Division with a 12–1–1 record, but because of a new playoff system, they found themselves again pitted against arch-rival Kansas City—the second-place finishers— for the AFL championship.

But this time Nemiah was far more than a spectator. With the Raiders ahead 7–0 after the first quarter, Kansas City quarterback Len Dawson at-

Wilson (48) and teammate Phil Villapiano bounce New York's Emerson Boozer on his head.

tempted to pass to his great All-Pro receiver Otis Taylor.

The ball was thrown low, however, and Wilson stepped in front of Taylor, appeared to pick the ball off right at his shoetop, and headed upfield with nothing in front of him but empty grass. "It was a touchdown all the way," Wilson said, "but one of the refs blew his whistle and said the ball had hit the ground before I caught it. I *know* I caught that ball. I cupped my hands just above the grass as I grabbed it. One ref said I did catch it, but he was overruled. And the ref who overruled him didn't blow his whistle until I started to run."

So instead of a 14–0 Oakland lead, which would probably have forced Kansas City to change its game plan, the score remained 7–0. Kansas City eventually won, 17–7, then went on to upset the heavily favored Minnesota Vikings in the Super Bowl.

The following year (1970) the American Football League merged with the National Football League. Three former NFL teams joined the original AFL clubs in what became the new American Football Conference. But things didn't change much for Wilson and his Raider teammates. Once again they edged the Chiefs and won the regular-season division championship. But again they were eliminated in the playoffs, this time losing the conference title game—and the chance to play in the Super Bowl— to the Baltimore Colts.

In 1971 the Raiders failed to win their division

crown for the first time in five years. In an incredible coincidence, another controversial referee's call on a play involving Kansas City's Otis Taylor and the Raiders' Nemiah Wilson contributed to Oakland's downfall.

When Kansas City and Oakland met before 51,215 screaming fans in Kansas City with two games to go in the 1971 regular season, the two clubs were almost tied for first place. Kansas City's record was 8–3–1, while Oakland's was 7–3–2. Obviously this was a crucial game for both teams.

Oakland led 14–9 with only a minute left to play. Once again, Kansas City quarterback Len Dawson looked for Otis Taylor, who was streaking far downfield accompanied by Wilson. "I stayed on the outside of him all the way because I knew I would have help covering him inside from the free safety," Wilson said. "Finally he tried to make a move to the outside and ran right into me. Would you believe the ref threw the flag on me for interference? It gave them a first down on the one-yard line, setting up their winning touchdown."

Final score: Kansas City 16, Oakland 14.

It wasn't the first time Oakland had been edged out of the big prize—nor was it the last. After recapturing their division championship in 1972, the Raiders met the Pittsburgh Steelers in the playoffs. With seconds to go Oakland led 7–6. But in the game's final play, Steeler quarterback Terry Bradshaw threw a desperation pass to receiver Ron

Wilson slows down Miami's speedy Mercury Morris during the 1973 AFC championship game.

Shanklin. The ball was jarred out of his hands, bounced off his shoetop on the fly—into the arms of Steeler Franco Harris, who raced 42 yards into the end zone for a game-winning touchdown just as the final gun went off. "In a million years I don't think you'll ever see a play like that again," Wilson said, speaking for all the stunned Raiders.

In 1973 the Raiders were back in the playoffs, but again they fell short of the top. This time they lost the AFC championship by a decisive 27–10 loss to the Miami Dolphins, and even their most partisan fans had to admit that the Raiders were beaten fairly and squarely.

There was only one thing the Oakland players could do—pick themselves up and start thinking about next year. Nemiah Wilson certainly wasn't ready to give up. Playing with perennial contenders, Wilson was seeing more action than he had ever dreamed of. And when you're 6 feet tall and weigh 165 pounds, that's half the battle already.

5.

Randy Vataha

The music blared "Whistle While You Work"
throughout the corner of Disneyland where the
Seven Little Dwarfs were doing their thing. But
under his heavy plastic mask of Bashful, Randy
Vataha was too hot and too tired to feel much like
whistling. It was July of 1968, and the young college
student was finding out that his new summer job
wasn't all fun and games.

On this particular day, however, Vataha got an
unexpected break from his taxing responsibilities as
a dwarf.

"The whole idea was pretty much to follow the
dwarf in front of you," he recalled. "I think I
followed Sneezy. People would take pictures of you,
little kids would touch you, and babies would cry at

The two faces of Randy Vataha: A smiling Randy (above) looks more like "Happy" than "Bashful" (below, far left).

you. But if something happened to one dwarf, all of us would have to go in because everyone would start asking, 'How come there's only six little dwarfs?'

"Well, this one real hot day—you'd really boil under that outfit—I looked over at my fellow dwarfs and one of them, I think it was Grumpy, took a headlong dive into this little pond where we worked. I don't know if he tripped over a little kid, or just got so hot he couldn't stand it, but in any case we all got a half day off."

It would have been a strange job for anyone, but for Randy Vataha, who played Bashful between his freshman and sophomore years at Golden West Junior College, it was positively bizarre. Just picture it—a rough, tough football star dressed up like one of the Seven Little Dwarfs! The answer, of course, is that Vataha wasn't all that rough and tough. He could more accurately be described as fast and tricky. At 5-foot-9 and 165 pounds, he had to be to survive the violence of the big man's game. Vataha not only survived, he eventually flourished as a fine pass catcher for the New England Patriots. Still, his long, bumpy climb to the top was as improbable as . . . well, as a Walt Disney fairy tale.

Born in Santa Maria, California, December 4, 1948, Randy moved to Long Beach when he was two and to Garden Grove when he was six. His father was a truck driver for an oil drilling company and his mother was a dental assistant. While they were far from wealthy, Vataha recalled, "We were never lacking for anything."

At the age of eight, Randy joined a Little League baseball team coached by his dad and got his first taste of organized sports. He didn't play football until his freshman year at Ranchos Alamitos High School, however, and even then he wasn't very enthusiastic. "The main reason I went out there was because all my friends were trying out," he said. "Baseball season wasn't until the spring so I said, 'What the heck, why not?'"

The freshman football coach made Vataha a running back. "I was pretty fast, and at that point all they did was line everyone up and see who was fastest," Randy explained. "The first two got to be the starting halfbacks."

Vataha was about 5-foot-7 and 150 pounds at the time—the last occasion he was anywhere near the same size of his teammates. In the next few years they grew lots, but Randy grew only a little.

As a sophomore he played defensive back and was the reserve quarterback for the junior varsity. In his junior year he started out as a running back with the varsity, but that changed after the first half of his first game.

"We were losing 20–0 near the end of the second quarter, and our quarterback wasn't doing so well," Vataha recalled. "So they put me in at quarterback. The first play I called was a quick pass. I was rushed pretty hard, so I just tried to throw the ball away deep. I didn't have the greatest arm, but we had this very good split end and . . . well, he ended up running across the field and catching it for a touchdown. I wound up being the starting quarterback thanks to a pass I tried to throw away."

Ranchos Alamitos tied for its league championship that year and won it outright the next. When the good-run, poor-throw little quarterback was named the league's Player of the Year as a senior, his future looked bright. "I told the coach that when the people from USC, Oklahoma, Notre Dame, and Nebraska showed up he should just line 'em up outside the door and we'd talk to them one by one," Vataha recalled with a rueful grin. But Randy was in for a rude shock. "As it wound up, I didn't get a single offer," he admitted. "After about a month I began to realize that most colleges aren't interested in a 155-pound quarterback who can't pass."

Vataha, who was an outstanding shortstop on the baseball team, did get a phone call from the New York Yankees, who wanted to know if he was interested in a pro baseball career. But Randy was determined to get a college education. Besides he had come to find baseball's slow pace dull, so he told the Yankees he wasn't interested. Right then and there he decided that if he was going anywhere in sports, it would be in football.

Fortunately, California football players who are at first rejected by the major colleges can still turn to the state's extensive system of excellent junior colleges. Many times a big school will tell a young player to go to a junior college, polish his skills, and then reapply. A large percentage of the players on the USC and UCLA teams in any given year started out at junior colleges. So Vataha enrolled at Golden West Junior College in Huntington Beach, California.

As a running back again, Randy had an excellent season as a freshman, finishing second in the conference in rushing. "But at the end of the year," he said, "my coach decided that at my size, if I was ever going to have a chance of playing major college ball, which is what I wanted to do, I would have to be either a wide receiver or a defensive back. I only weighed 160 or 165, and there was no way I could have taken the pounding a running back takes in major college play. The coach said he'd switch me if I agreed. I did. Since I'd always played on offense, we decided on wide receiver.

"I remember how terrible I was in our scrimmage the week before the first game after I moved to wide receiver. I had three passes bounce off my chest. I just couldn't do anything right. Looking back, I'm very grateful that the coach didn't put me back at running back where he knew I'd be useful to the team."

In time Randy became useful at his new position, too—to put it mildly. He set a state record for receptions, catching more than 50 in nine games, and made first team junior college All-America. Lots of big colleges were now interested in the little receiver, and eventually Randy narrowed his choice down to three—Stanford, Oklahoma, and Utah.

He finally chose Stanford mainly for its excellent academic standing, but also because it was relatively close to home. To top it all off, quarterback Jim Plunkett had just completed an outstanding sophomore season there as a passer—a good sign for any receiver. "I knew Stanford would throw the ball," explained Vataha.

Jim Plunkett met Randy at the airport when he arrived at Stanford, the start of a continuing collaboration between passer and receiver. "I had asked how I would recognize Plunkett," Randy recalled, "and they told me to look for a guy who looked like an athlete. When I got off the plane, there was Jim in his blue levis and Stanford letterman's jacket, and I knew who he was immediately."

The season before Vataha arrived Plunkett's favorite target had been 6-foot-1, 185-pound Gene Washington, who went on to stardom with the San Francisco 49ers. Getting used to throwing to the far smaller Vataha wasn't easy for Plunkett, who observed that "Randy looked like he was running in a ditch."

Randy himself was so self-conscious about his small size that he asked Stanford sports information director Bob Murphy to list him on the program as 5-foot-10 and 175 pounds, cheating by at least ten pounds and an inch or so. But the director knew better. "One day I told him, 'I'm tired of fooling the public, get on that scale,'" Murphy said. "Randy

At Stanford, Randy grabs a Jim Plunkett TD pass against UCLA.

looked around to be sure no one was watching and stepped on the scale. He weighed 163."

Vataha may have been small, but he could run and he could fake and he could catch a football in a crowd. In his two seasons at Stanford he was their leading receiver. He caught 35 passes for 691 yards and five touchdowns in 1969, and did even better the next year when he grabbed 48 passes for 844 yards and six touchdowns.

The two biggest single thrills of Vataha's college career were beating USC in his senior year (a game in which Randy's nine receptions sparked the first Stanford victory over the Trojans in 13 years) and beating Ohio State in the 1970 Rose Bowl.

"It's hard to describe what it's like to play in the Rose Bowl," Vataha said. "The biggest thing is the tradition involved. I know I've watched the Rose Bowl ever since I can remember watching television. Then when you get into the game and you go to all the banquets before the game and you hear stories about the 1936 game and the 1945 game and so forth, you realize you're taking part in something very few football players get the opportunity to participate in."

Randy added his own chapter to Rose Bowl history by catching the touchdown pass that clinched Stanford's 27–17 victory. He had run several deep, outside patterns against his Ohio State defender. On the big scoring play, he faked the deep outside move, the defender went for the fake, and Vataha hooked back toward the line of scrimmage.

As he turned, Plunkett's bullet spiral arrived, a textbook example of the perfect timing a passer and receiver strive for.

Even though he'd had two outstanding seasons at Stanford, Vataha was still dwarf-sized by pro standards. He wasn't drafted by the pros until the Los Angeles Rams took a chance on him way down in the 17th round—when most teams admit they are simply stabbing in the dark. But Vataha wasn't really surprised by the pros' lack of interest.

"I wasn't counting on being drafted at all," he explained. "I knew my size was against me. Of course, you always think that somewhere, sometime, a pro coach had seen you play and decided to take a chance on you, but by no means did I have my heart set on a pro career."

The Rams were set at wide receiver with standout veterans Jack Snow and Lance Rentzel. They also had a third receiver, Pat Studstill, a proven pro who did double duty as the Rams' punter. So Vataha wasn't given much of a chance to show what he could do. In the opening exhibition of 1971 Randy caught a touchdown pass against Houston. But he wasn't thrown to again in the next three games, and before the regular season even began, he was cut by the Rams.

"I had prepared myself the best I could," he said. "I had worked out for about two and a half months with the Rams because I lived near where they trained. I really thought I might be crushed if I was cut because I had never failed before, but it's funny that when it happened I wasn't really that disappointed. I didn't feel I had failed because there simply wasn't anything else I could have done to succeed. I gave it my best shot, so I had nothing to feel sorry about. My family and friends couldn't believe it. They kept staring at me, wondering when I'd fall down on the carpet and throw a fit."

The experience was just another example of a hard fact of football life Vataha had already learned —the little guy never gets the benefit of the doubt in the minds of coaches. "A lot of times they'll stick with a guy who's 6-foot-2 because they think he has a lot of potential," he said. "But for some reason they look at a guy my size and say, 'Okay, this is what he can do,' and that's it. They never think in terms of me getting better. That's why the little man almost has to find a team that needs him right away."

Vataha waited a few days after the Rams gave him the bad news to see if any other team showed any interest in him. None did, so he took a short vacation in Las Vegas and then returned home to plan a nonfootball future.

But Vataha's football days weren't over yet. Without his knowing it, the Rams had told the New England Patriots he might be worth a look. The Patriots, in turn, had asked the opinion of an obviously well-informed source, their rookie quarterback Jim Plunkett. Plunkett said he thought his old sidekick was at least as good as any receiver the Patriots had then.

So nine days after being cut by Los Angeles Vataha got a call from the Patriots. "Jerry Stoltz, the receiver coach, asked if I was interested in trying out," Vataha recalled. "I said, 'Great, I'd love to. I'm still in good shape. When do you want me to fly out?'

"He said, 'Well, we're not sure we want you to try out. We just want to see if you're interested.' Then he said he'd call back the next day.

"The next day I got a call around seven in the morning. The Patriots said that if I wanted to try out, I should make a nine o'clock flight out of Los Angeles. I hadn't packed anything and it's a 45-minute ride to the airport. We raced around like crazy and tore down the San Diego Freeway, but I missed the plane by about five minutes. I could see the plane on the runway, and I was telling the lady at the counter I had to get on—that I was going for a tryout with the New England Patriots. Somehow, I don't think she believed me.

"I called the Patriots back and said, 'Well, I really appreciated the chance but I just couldn't make it.' They said, 'Okay, take the twelve o'clock flight.'"

Vataha arrived in Boston only a week and a half before the start of the season. But the Patriots were very weak at wide receiver, and Randy caught on to their system fast. He got into the second half of the first regular-season game, caught a 40-yard pass from his old friend Plunkett, and was on his way to what he called "a pinch-me-is-this-really-happening type of season."

Vataha was an immediate favorite with the Patriot fans, who started calling him "Rabbit" because of the way he scurried downfield and darted away from defenders. His 51 receptions tied a New England club record, and they were good for 872 yards, an eye-popping average of 17.1 yards per catch, and nine touchdowns.

As a rookie, Vataha got one of the best birthday presents ever. He and Plunkett were born just a day apart, and on December 5, 1971, they staged a real celebration. With signs saying "Happy Birthday, Jim and Randy," all over the Patriots' stadium, the two combined for seven completions in a startling upset of the powerful Miami Dolphins.

They carried out two 30-yard "hook and go" touchdown strikes that day. Twice Vataha scampered downfield, suddenly slammed on the brakes, and turned. Plunkett raised his arm and pumped. The Dolphin defender raced up, anticipating the pass, but Vataha suddenly turned and took off again, leaving the poor cornerback all alone. No one was near the Rabbit when he clutched the football to his chest in the end zone. It was an old, familiar pass pattern, but they made it look new.

In the 1971 season finale against the Baltimore Colts Vataha caught four passes, two for touchdowns. One of the scoring passes, an 88-yarder, set a Patriot team record. "We were ahead by about three

Randy catches another touchdown pass from Plunkett—this time for the Patriots in a 1971 upset of the Miami Dolphins.

points, and it was third and eight from our own twelve-yard line," he recalled. "They expected us to run. Jim called a play-action pass [a pass that starts off looking like a run] and the cornerback came up. Jim dropped back and released the ball, and it came right over the top of my helmet into my arms. There wasn't anyone within ten yards of me when I caught it. I just coasted down the field. It's hard to describe how great that feels."

Vataha's rookie season couldn't have been better, but the next year was, in his own words, "a disaster." His receptions dropped to 25, his yardage to 369, and his touchdowns to two.

There were several reasons for the decline. First of all, defenses that had perhaps underestimated him as a rookie began to pay much more attention to him in 1972. Secondly, his attitude was not what it should have been. "I was too confident," he admitted. "I had a big head, I guess. I'd had a pretty good rookie year and I thought I had it made."

Finally, conflicts within the Patriots' organization were causing problems for the entire team. "We had a general manager who fired the coach," Vataha explained. "But the owner rehired him—but only with a one-year contract. The coach was mad at the general manager for trying to fire him and mad at the owner for only giving him a one-year contract. The general manager was mad at the coach because he wanted to fire him and mad at the owner because he wouldn't let him fire him. And the owner was

mad at everybody. And through the whole thing everyone kept telling the public, 'No, nobody is mad at anybody.' Of course, all this conflict filtered down to the team. It was just a bad year for everyone."

Vataha began the 1973 season with a much better attitude. "I showed my first year I was capable of a good year," he said. "I showed my second year I was capable of a bad year. Now that I know I'm capable of both, I've taken steps to make sure which one it will be."

It wasn't quite that easy, though. Vataha got sick in training camp, suffering from stomach ailments and severe chest pains. The doctors never did figure out what was wrong with him, and it took a month before he was completely well. By that time Reggie Rucker and rookie Darryl Stingley, a first-round draft choice, were playing ahead of him. But gradually, Randy worked his way back into the line-up, alternating with the other two receivers. Playing only part-time, he still finished the season with 20 receptions for 341 yards and two touchdowns.

"And I improved my blocking a hundred—no, two hundred—percent," he said, beaming at a new found skill usually reserved for the game's big men. "I feel like I'm back to where I was. The coaches have confidence in my ability again and it showed on the field."

For a man who had once played a dwarf, Randy Vataha was looking bigger every day.

Vataha eludes a Detroit Lion tackler.

6.

Pat Fischer

More than ten years after it happened, Pat Fischer still vividly recalled his first meeting with John David Crow. Crow stood 6-foot-2 and weighed 220 pounds, every one of them rock-hard muscle. A paralyzed nerve made one side of his face droop, turning one corner of his mouth down in a constant grimace. Fully outfitted in his shoulder, hip, and thigh pads, the great running star of the St. Louis Cardinals looked like a man you would not want to meet in a dark alley. For that matter, if he was as mean as he looked (which he wasn't), you wouldn't want to meet him anywhere.

Rookie Pat Fischer was 5-foot-9 and weighed just 170 pounds. In fact, he was so small that the Cardinals didn't have a helmet or pads to fit him. At

Cardinal Pat Fischer (37) breaks up a touchdown pass intended for Gary Collins of the Cleveland Browns.

the time Fischer was an obscure 17th-round draft choice from Nebraska who was given only the barest outside chance of making the team.

The two men met on an open field during the first Cardinal scrimmage of the 1961 training camp. Crow was rumbling upfield with the ball, an awesome combination of muscle and speed. Suddenly, Fischer veered into his path.

It looked like a battle between a destroyer and a tugboat. But to the surprise of Crow and everyone watching along the sidelines, the little tug proved to be incredibly well armed. After a tremendous collision, Crow felt himself being lifted and thrown back on his rear end. And in that instant, little Pat Fischer's chances of becoming a pro football player improved 100 percent.

But Fischer wasn't the kind of man to take anything for granted. In fact, he didn't believe he had a real chance of becoming a Cardinal until weeks later. He was much too cautious and too modest to think he had it made before he got official notification. But that was nothing new. Four years earlier as an All-State high school star he had refused to believe he would get a scholarship to the University of Nebraska until the school actually offered him one. Then, despite a fine college career, Fischer didn't think he'd be drafted until the actual call came from the Cardinals.

"Peering into the future is something we all do," Fischer said, "but I really believe it's fruitless. I read that a long time ago and it made sense to me, so I try not to do it. As a result, I don't think I have ever been disappointed in my athletic career. Until someone says, 'You've got it, here it is,' I try not to anticipate."

He may have been wary of anticipating how far he would eventually go in the sport, but even cautious Pat Fischer always knew that he would play football. He was raised in the kind of home where a baby Fischer boy slept with a football in his crib. After having three daughters, the Fischers had six sons— Cletis, Kenny, Rex, Jack, Pat, and Jerry. All the Fischer boys played football and all attended the University of Nebraska. Cletis, Kenny, and Rex, the older Fischer brothers, had established a statewide reputation in football, "so the younger boys grew up thinking of playing the game," explained Pat.

With the exception of 6-foot-1, 215-pound Jack, all the brothers were on the small side—under 6-feet and less than 200 pounds. Still, Cletis went on to play one season with the New York Giants before becoming assistant coach at the University of Nebraska; Kenny was athletic director and head football coach of a high school in Nebraska; Rex, an All-Conference halfback at the university, was drafted by the San Francisco 49ers but chose medicine instead of football as his profession. And, of course, Pat became one of the finest cornerbacks in the National Football League, first with the Cardinals and then with the Washington Redskins.

Pat Fischer was born in St. Edward, Nebraska, on January 2, 1940. His dad was a carpenter, and although the family was far from rich, Pat thought his childhood was ideal. "St. Edward might have been even smaller than it sounds," he said with a laugh. "I don't think the population has ever exceeded 1,000. But I was extremely happy there.

"All the little boys in the community knew each other. You'd get up out of bed, get dressed, and run two or three blocks and there were all the other kids your age either playing ball or swimming in the town pool. You'd play baseball in the morning, then when the pool opened at 12 o'clock, you'd go dive in. When you got tired of that, it was back to the ballfield.

"It was a boy's dream. Everything was there. We had two or three little rivers where you could go fishing. When you got older, you could go hunting. We played ball all day long. Whatever sport was in season, that's what we'd play. You could always find someone willing to play. We had all the fun you wish all children had a chance to enjoy."

When Pat was in the sixth grade the Fischers moved 150 miles to Oakland, Nebraska, where Pat's dad found work at some large government projects that were being built. Not so coincidentally, Oakland also happened to be where Kenny had taken his first job as a head high school coach. Brother Rex, a junior then, became Kenny's first star.

Pat played for Kenny as a freshman and a

sophomore. "I loved it, even though he was tougher on me than anyone else," Pat recalled. "After my sophomore year we moved to Omaha, and Kenny took another job in Chappel, Nebraska. I didn't want to move to Omaha. I wanted to go to Chappel with Kenny."

But Pat went to Omaha, where he made All-State in football as a running back at Westside High School. He also found time for basketball, baseball, and track.

There never was any question about where he wanted to go to college. "Nebraska boys dreamed about playing for the state university and beating Oklahoma," explained Fischer, referring to one of college football's great traditional rivalries. And of course the Fischer boys had their own tradition when it came to the University of Nebraska.

Pat received invitations to visit several other schools, but he had his heart set on Nebraska. Still, Fischer wasn't at all sure that Nebraska wanted him. "Up until they offered the grant-in-aid, I was apprehensive," he said. "I was hopeful, but until they offered it I couldn't be absolutely sure."

As a sophomore in 1958, Fischer made his Nebraska varsity debut, returning a punt 92 yards for a touchdown against Penn State. The following year, he had his boyhood wish fulfilled when Nebraska beat Oklahoma 25–21 to snap Oklahoma's 13-year, 74-game Big 8 Conference winning streak. Fischer returned a punt 70 yards to Oklahoma's one-yard

Fischer catches his breath after a tough play.

line to set up a key touchdown in that momentous victory.

In his senior year Fischer's Nebraska team again beat Oklahoma 17–14. "And we beat 'em that time at Norman [Oklahoma] after trailing 14–0 at the half," Pat recalled, still proud of the victory.

Fischer played quarterback and halfback at Nebraska, returned punts and kickoffs for the special teams, and even played in the secondary on defense because college substitutions were limited in those days.

Fischer had a fine college career, but he was by no means a superstar. He did not make All-America. He didn't even make the All-Conference team. What he did do was rush 229 times for 801 yards, an average of 3.5 yards per carry. He passed 51 times, completing 14 for 252 yards and one touchdown. He also returned 31 kickoffs for 786 yards, an average of 25.3 yards per return, and ran back 30 punts for 550 yards, an average of 18 yards per return.

Despite his collegiate achievements, Fischer was not counting on a football future. "Someone told me I probably wouldn't be drafted because I was too small," he recalled. "But at that time I never even dreamed of playing pro ball. Heck, I was a fan. I had no idea of how good I was. Pro football seemed so far above me."

For that matter, even being in the company of some of the country's top college stars awed the modest Fischer. He was thrilled at being named a starter in the Miami North-South All-Star game, an annual exhibition designed to give pro scouts a final look at the best college prospects.

In that game Fischer intercepted one pass, knocked down several others, and made believers of the Dallas Texans of the American Football League (now the Kansas City Chiefs), the Cardinals, and Calgary of the Canadian Football League. He signed with St. Louis, but in typical Fischer fashion, didn't expect much when he left for his first training camp. He still needed a few more credits to graduate from college, and he still expected to get them. "I accepted the Cardinals' proposal," he explained, "knowing that if I was cut—and for some reason I just assumed I would be cut—I would be back at Nebraska in plenty of time to enroll."

Fischer never did go back to school. As a Cardinal rookie in 1961, he played on all the special teams, returning punts and defending against opponents' kickoff and punt returns. He had his eye on winning a regular job but, of course, he refused to look ahead that far. "I enjoyed the special teams," he recalled. "If that's all you're allowed to do, you'd best do it well."

The special teams in pro football used to be called the suicide squads—for good reason. When you get eleven young, strong, ambitious giants running from one end of the field as fast as they can toward an identical eleven heading the other way, you are bound to get some bone-rattling collisions.

The little rookie's place in such violent doings seemed particularly suicidal, but Fischer showed little concern. "Fear is not part of the game," he said. "Football is violent, but if you're well prepared you have nothing to fear. I had fine teachers and was very well trained. Anyone who feels fear is not going to have the proper timing and confidence, and without those two elements you're simply not going to be successful. The game is one of angles. If you take the proper angle of pursuit, you're going to be in the proper position to make contact. It's as simple as that."

Fischer started at cornerback the first four games of 1962, his second season, but a torn hamstring muscle sidelined him for the rest of the year. At the start of 1963 Fischer was in danger of losing his hard-won toe hold in the NFL. "I was playing less than the field-goal kicker," he recalled. "I told coach [Wally] Lemm, 'Put me in and keep me in—or bench me.' He benched me."

An injury had put Fischer in peril, and ironically it was another injury that saved his career. Regular Cardinal cornerback Jimmy Hill got hurt just before St. Louis was scheduled to meet the Bears in Chicago. The Cardinals had played in Chicago before the franchise was moved to St. Louis, and there was nothing the Cards' management enjoyed more than beating their former city rivals, particularly in Chicago.

"Lemm had a choice of playing me or a rookie,"

Fischer recalled. "He figured he'd better go with me, knowing how badly his bosses wanted to win that game."

After playing well against the Bears, Fischer was put back in the regular line-up. He went on to intercept eight passes and return them 169 yards, second best in the NFL for 1963. The next year he intercepted ten passes and returned them for 164 yards and two touchdowns, again ranking second in the league.

The highlight of 1964 was a late-season game against Pittsburgh. With four minutes to play, Fischer grabbed a fumble in midair and returned it 49 yards for a touchdown that gave St. Louis a 21–20 victory. It was the Cardinals' first win in Pittsburgh in 17 years—but more important, it kept them in contention for the NFL's Eastern Division championship. The Cards (9–3–2) eventually were nosed out for the title by Cleveland (10–3–1), but without Fischer they wouldn't even have had a chance. In the Playoff Bowl between the second-place teams in the Eastern and Western Conferences, Pat scored three touchdowns in a victory over Green Bay, was chosen the Cardinals' Most Valuable Player of the season, and was named All-Pro.

As Pat perfected his knowledge and skills at cornerback, he became known as one of the very best at his position. He was an NFL All-Star in 1964 and 65 and missed in 66 only because a knee injury kept him out of action for half the season. The

Cardinals, unfortunately, weren't doing nearly as well.

The 1966 season was particularly frustrating. The Cardinals got off to a great start with five wins in a row, but then quarterback Charley Johnson was injured and they only won two of their remaining eight games.

In 1967 the Cardinals sank to a 6–7–1 record, and internal dissension wracked the team. After the Dallas Cowboys passed St. Louis silly in a 46–21 Thanksgiving rout, coach Charley Winner blasted Fischer and the other Card cornerback, Jimmy Burson. The two defensive backs, in turn, blamed a

Fischer intercepts a pass against Pittsburgh before being tackled by the intended receiver, Clenden Thomas.

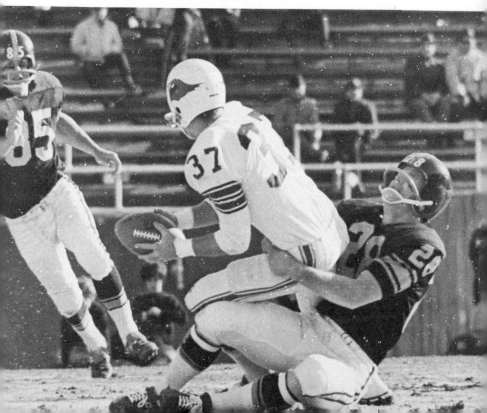

weak Cardinal pass rush for their problems, pointing out that if a passer has enough time, he can hit his receivers no matter who is trying to defend against them. This angry exchange and a salary dispute he was having with the management completely soured Fischer on the Cardinals.

In the summer of '68 he was signed by the Washington Redskins, who paid the Cardinals a second- and third-round draft choice as compensation. Redskins' coach Bill Austin explained his interest in Fischer. "At first glance, he has none of the pro requirements," Austin said. "He's too short, too light, too slow. All he can do is play left cornerback like very few people can."

Few men knew more about playing cornerback than Pat Fischer. "A cornerback's primary responsibility is to defend against split ends or receivers that are split away from the line of scrimmage," he explained. "I think it's that additional part of professional football that separates it from college ball—the passing game. With those two wide receivers, teams can move the ball downfield in a big hurry, gaining substantial amounts of real estate in a very short time. I think it's the part where the game is won and lost.

"To be able to play cornerback properly is a matter basically of being able to run and react backward. You run backward at least ten or fifteen yards as that receiver accelerates from the line of scrimmage. It's a duel.

Playing for the Washington Redskins, Pat wrestles with Cowboy Bob Hayes for the ball, which is just above their heads.

"A receiver starts every year in training camp as I do, running patterns, trying to shift his weight and add speed to change directions. A cornerback has to train himself to look at films and run the same patterns that the receiver does, only in reverse. If he's going to run an 'out' pattern [a few yards downfield followed by a sharp cut to the sideline], what does he do every time as he releases from the line of scrimmage that can tell you that's the pattern? Is he skipping, is he moving inside out, or does he move outside in? Where is he trying to get in relation to where you are in order to make that pattern work? How much speed can he maintain when he changes direction—it differs between a man who's 6-foot-4 and one 5-foot-10, and it makes the pattern look entirely different to you even though the two are running the same play. It's not as simple as it looks from the stands or on TV."

For three also-ran seasons, life with the Redskins was depressingly similar to Fischer's Cardinal career. But in 1971 dynamic George Allen left the Los Angeles Rams to become Washington's head coach and general manager, and almost overnight, the Skins became contenders. Allen immediately started to assemble what came to be called "The Over the Hill Gang," trading draft choices for proven veterans. Some thought the men he acquired were too old—thus the nickname—but Allen had the last laugh. The 1971 Redskins finished with a 9–4–1 record, their best mark in 26 years, and made the playoffs before a 24–20 loss to San Francisco ended their season.

In 1972 the Redskins won the National Football Conference's Eastern Division crown with an 11–3 record. Then they defeated Green Bay and Dallas in the playoffs to win the conference championship and qualify for the Super Bowl. Their 14–7 loss to Miami was a disappointing end to a glorious season, but it couldn't keep all of Washington, including the President of the United States, from exulting over the thrill of their team's getting that far after so many years of futility. And no one appreciated the feeling of accomplishment more than Pat Fischer, who had spent many of his own years on the losing side.

"The game of football has always been thrilling, but now there's an additional dimension—the overall team's success," Fischer explained. "It doesn't take you long to realize that that's the goal, that's really what you're looking for. The personal rewards the game has given me are nowhere near the thrill of when the entire team is recognized for its achievement and you can say, 'Well, I did my part.' That's the greatest thrill."

In 1973 the Redskins were back in the heat of the race. Their 10–4 record qualified them for the playoffs against the Minnesota Vikings. The Skins took a 7–3 lead into the half time intermission and were tied 10–10 going into the fourth quarter. But then the Vikings' veteran quarterback Fran Tarken-

Fischer (37) and Redskin teammate Roosevelt Taylor knock the ball away from Dallas' Lance Alworth in the 1972 NFC title game.

ton threw two touchdown passes to wide receiver John Gilliam in the game's final 15 minutes. Guarded by Fischer, Gilliam had not hurt the Redskins through three quarters, but the gritty little Redskin defender had cracked his ribs making a tackle in the second quarter and eventually had to come out. "He attempted to continue to play, but it was just too painful," said George Allen after the game. "His loss was extremely costly."

In fact, the cornerback's loss cost the Redskins the championship. Gilliam's two scoring catches against Fischer's replacement gave the Vikings their 27–20 victory.

Less than two weeks after that game Fischer celebrated his 34th birthday, which made him a senior citizen by pro football standards. But when asked about retirement he gave a typical Fischer answer.

"I'll give up when my feet flatly refuse to run," said Fischer. "Why retire if you can still run? I have no preconceived plans. I try not to peer into the future."

7.

Harold Jackson

He looked like just another skinny little boy as he ran down the street from the grocery store toward home. But in his own mind, young Harold Jackson was a football star racing faster than the wind, scoring a touchdown before thousands of cheering fans.

"Running was kind of the thing to do in my neighborhood as a kid," explained Jackson, one of six children who grew up in Hattiesburg, Mississippi. "If Mama asked you to go to the store for a loaf of bread, you ran to the store. Then you ran back, carrying that loaf of bread like it was a football. We were always playing little games like who could run three or four blocks the fastest. It was something big to be the fastest. About sixth grade, I think, I finally made fastest."

131

Years later, many people thought Jackson was still the fastest runner in the neighborhood. But by then his neighborhood was the National Football League, and the touchdowns he scored were real, not just dreams. Overcoming his lack of size with dedication, intelligence, and above all, blazing speed, the 5-foot-11, 170-pound Jackson became one of pro football's greatest pass receivers. But Jackson's road to stardom was bumpy because he constantly had to prove that someone so small could succeed in a big man's game.

His parents were the first people he had to convince. The Jacksons once went to a varsity game at Hattiesburg's Rowan High School, noted the size and ferocity of the players, and told their son (who weighed only 130 pounds at the time) to join the band. For two years the only time Harold stepped into the end zone was at half time. And then he had a trumpet—not a football—in his hands.

Jackson did play football in gym class, however, and his mother wasn't very happy about that. "I'd come home with my knees ripped out of my pants," he recalled, "and Mama would say, 'No more football.' Next day my knees would be out again and Mama would just throw up her hands."

Jackson showed such football talent in gym that the teachers encouraged him to try out for the

Harold Jackson relaxes on the sidelines.

varsity. Realizing how badly he wanted to play, his parents finally gave their approval. Harold had no trouble making the team, and he soon became an outstanding player.

By his senior year, college scouts were in the stands watching every game. Eventually, the choice narrowed down to two schools—Jackson State and Florida A&M. He finally chose to attend Jackson State. The school was just 90 miles from Hattiesburg, far closer to home than Florida A&M. But that was only part of the reason he wound up there.

Harold Jackson smiled as he recounted the trick Jackson State pulled to lure him away from its rival. "It was a Thursday night—I never forget the night," he recalled. "That weekend I was scheduled to make a trip to the campus at Florida A&M. My folks and I were sitting on the porch talking about it when this car pulled up. It was a couple of coaches from Jackson State. They said that I would have to go on up to Jackson and take this test. They said it was very important. Well, I ended up staying through the whole weekend while they kept showing me what a great school Jackson State was. I ain't taken the test yet."

Jackson State was one of a number of Southern schools with predominantly black student bodies that year after year turn out some of the finest football players in the country. Jackson State had just sent Willie Richardson, its great pass catcher, to professional stardom with the Baltimore Colts. And during Harold's senior year eleven Jackson State players were drafted by the pros—a figure rivaled only by the much bigger and better known Southern California.

So, as good as he was, Harold had plenty of competition when he began his college career. He finally got a chance to show what he could do when a receiver named Taft Reed (who was later drafted by the Philadelphia Eagles) got hurt. From then on, Jackson State's starting pass catchers were Gloster Richardson, Willie's brother and a future member of the Kansas City Chiefs, and a 149-pounder who wore No. 00, Harold Jackson. Reed never got his job back. Once he was healthy again, he was switched to defensive back.

That was the beginning of a brilliant college career for Harold Jackson. He went on to break all of Willie Richardson's pass-catching records and professional stardom seemed the next logical step. In his senior year pro scouts gathered to watch Jackson every week, just as the college bird dogs had flocked to see him four years earlier at Rowan High. Then, suddenly, they disappeared. There was nothing more for them to look at. Jackson suffered a partially torn knee ligament, an injury that put him in a cast for six weeks and scared off the scouts. Without sound legs, Jackson's football value was nil. "Guess they thought I was washed up," he said.

But coach George Allen of the Los Angeles Rams figured Harold was still worth a gamble and selected

Pursued by a Dallas defender, Jackson speeds to the Ram end zone.

him on the 14th round of the 1968 draft.

Jackson played in only two regular-season games during his rookie year. He spent most of his time on the Rams' taxi squad, as one of seven players who practiced with the regular team during the week but didn't suit up for the Sunday games unless one of the regulars was injured.

During the weekly practices, it was Jackson's job to imitate the speediest pass receiver of the Rams' upcoming opponent so that the Rams could practice their defense. "One week I would be Bob Hayes, the next week Clifton NcNeil, and the next week Paul Warfield," Jackson recalled. "I was always the fastest man on the other team."

Others might have resented such treatment, but Jackson never did. "Coach Allen took a chance when he drafted me out of college after I got hurt," Harold explained. "He also helped me prepare for the complicated defenses I would face in the NFL. Every day after practice, he would show me how to get around the linebackers and by the free safety. Jack Pardee, one of our linebackers, would cut me down and try to block me, but in the long run it helped me."

Still, as his rookie season progressed and he continued to do nothing but pretend to be other receivers, Jackson began to worry about his own future. One day, after working against Rams' defensive back Irv Cross in practice, the two men discussed the subject.

"With your moves, Harold, you've got to make it somewhere in this league," said Cross, who after months of chasing his teammate in practice knew just how good Jackson was.

"Uh-huh," Harold grunted. "But where?"

The next year Jackson got his answer. On July 7, 1969, he and defensive end John Zook were traded to Philadelphia for running back Izzy Lang.

Ironically, Irv Cross had a lot to do with that trade. During negotiations between Los Angeles and Philadelphia, George Allen gave Eagles' general manager Pete Retzlaff a list of fringe Ram players that he was willing to part with. Retzlaff showed that list to Cross, who by then had become an assistant Eagles coach.

Cross' eyes lit up when he saw Jackson's name. "Take Jackson," he told Retzlaff. "Believe me, Pete, he can fly."

"Then why would Allen let him go?" Retzlaff asked.

"He likes his receivers 6-foot-3 and 215 pounds," replied Cross. "Jackson's small, but he can motor."

"Your quarterbacks might have trouble reaching him," Cross jokingly told Eagles' offensive coach Charlie Grauer—but that turned out not to be much of a joke.

When Jackson reported to the Eagles that summer of 1969, he came straight from a six-month Army Reserve hitch, so he wasn't in top condition. Nevertheless, he quickly dazzled his new teammates with

his blazing speed. Until they adjusted to Jackson, the
Eagle passers constantly underthrew him simply
because they couldn't believe any human being
could get downfield that fast. Jackson honestly
didn't think it was possible to overthrow him. "If a

Playing for the Philadelphia Eagles in 1972, Jackson (29) loses control of the ball in the end zone.

quarterback is trying to hit the target, I don't think he can do it," he said. "But if he is just trying to throw the ball for distance, he might."

Retzlaff said, "Right now, considering their ages, I think Jackson can outrun Bob Hayes." Having his running ability even compared to that of Hayes was high praise, indeed, for Hayes was an Olympic sprint champion and a co-world record holder for the 100-yard dash. Although his track days were long behind him, many still considered Hayes to be the fastest man in the world.

"Did he say that?" asked Jackson with a giggle when told about Retzlaff's remark. "Well, I'll give him a go for the money."

In his very first scrimmage with Philadelphia, Jackson caught two 60-yard bombs from quarterback Norm Snead, immediately making a fan. "I know one thing," said Snead. "On a deep post, it's going to be hard to overthrow this kid."

And it was. The Eagles were a terrible team during the four seasons Jackson played with them, finishing last in their division three times and third once. Jackson was an immediate and spectacular success. He caught 65 passes for a league-leading 1,116 yards and nine touchdowns in 1969, 41 passes for 613 yards and five touchdowns in 1970, 47 passes for 716 yards and three touchdowns in 1971, and a league-leading 62 passes for a league-leading 1,048 yards and four touchdowns in 1972. No NFL receiver caught as many passes for as many yards in those four years. None even came close.

Jackson's great natural talent was one reason for his success, but not the only one. He also spent hours studying films of other great receivers and their techniques—the way former Baltimore Colt star Ray Berry stopped on a dime to catch a ball just before going out of bounds, for example, and the way ex-San Diego All-Pro Lance Alworth could charge across the middle, fake with his head and shoulders, leap, catch the ball, and hang on despite a jolting tackle by the defender.

"When I first came into the league every play was a footrace," Jackson explained. "To catch a pass, I had to outrun a defender. Now I try to do two things, outrun them and outthink them."

In addition to his natural talent and his diligent studies, Jackson also knew how to stay healthy. "I've never really had my bell rung in this game because I'm constantly rolling with the blows," he said. "I'm not a big target for the linebackers. I don't give them much to shoot at. The defensive back might get one good shot at me a game, but never three or four."

Healthy, intelligent, and magnificently talented, Jackson made some mind-boggling catches for the lowly Eagles. In a 1969 game, quarterback Snead was being tackled by 260-pound Dallas Cowboy All-Pro tackle Bob Lilly. Snead heaved a towering desperation bomb way down the middle of the field. Cowboy defensive backs Cornell Green and Mel Renfro converged, their eyes aglow in anticipation of an easy interception. Suddenly, seemingly out of nowhere, Harold Jackson flashed between them. He grabbed the ball, bounced off the two Dallas defenders, miraculously kept his balance, and staggered backward into the end zone to complete a 65-yard touchdown pass.

Another time, Jackson gave a classic demonstration of his ability to both outrun and outthink his man. The Eagles were playing the Giants in the final game of the 1971 season. Philadelphia quarterback Pete Liske called "56 from the round formation." Jackson, the primary receiver, dictated his own pattern according to the movement of the weak safety man, Richmond Flowers. Usually, the safety will protect deep, in which case Jackson tries to get open by running a short curl pattern in front of him. But Flowers, anticipating the play, came up. Jackson looped behind him and caught a 63-yard scoring pass. Not even Flowers, a world-class hurdler while at Tennessee, could gain ground on Jackson once the play became a match race.

By 1972 opponents began to realize that if they stopped Jackson, they'd have an excellent chance of stopping the Eagles because Philadelphia simply didn't have any other dangerous offensive threats. During the first eight games of the season, the Eagles had scored a total of only six touchdowns, and three of them were made by Jackson. Noting this, the St. Louis Cardinals decided to cover the fleet little receiver with everything they had.

"One guy told me he was talking to the St. Louis coaches," Jackson said later, "and they said if they could shut me off, they could stop our offense. They concentrated their whole game on me."

"They had one linebacker lined up right on Harold," explained Philadelphia's Pete Liske, "and the cornerback played him deep to the outside. They took everything away from our wide receivers. Most of our completions were to our tight ends and our backs."

"The linebacker went almost as deep as I did most plays," Jackson said. "I looked for him to come out, brush me, and let me go. But he stayed on me to shut off the short sideline pass. Then the cornerback played me almost man-to-man. Anytime I tried to go between them, the safetyman would come over on me. That was three guys I had to beat out there. Everytime the ball was snapped, the whole defense started rotating toward me."

Jackson was held to one 13-yard reception that day. But, as his season total of 62 receptions indicates, not many teams were able to neutralize Jackson so successfully. Still, he wished he could play for a team with a well-balanced offense that would make it impossible for opposing defenses to concentrate so heavily on him. And, like all athletes, he longed for the chance to play for a winner.

In June, 1973, both of his wishes came true. The Eagles traded Jackson, running back Tony Baker and two draft choices to the Los Angeles Rams for quarterback Roman Gabriel. Harold Jackson was

Jackson shows he's glad to be back in L. A. in 1973. In one game against the Dallas Cowboys he hauls in four passes —good for four touchdowns.

going back where he started from—but this time he would come to Los Angeles as an All-Pro instead of an untried rookie.

The Rams had the balanced offense and the winning record Jackson desired. He and quarterback John Hadl quickly established themselves as pro football's most explosive passing combination. On October 14, the two burned the powerful Dallas Cowboys for touchdown passes of 67, 63, 36, and 16 yards. In all, Jackson caught seven passes for 238 yards, one of the finest single-game performances by a receiver in NFL history. "Harold is definitely the best deep receiving threat in the league," said Hadl. "He has fantastic hands, fantastic speed, and a fantastic ability to get in the open."

That season Jackson caught 40 passes for 874 yards (21.9 per catch) and led the league with 13 touchdowns. "There's no big secret to it," he explained. "I just run as fast as I can downfield and Hadl lays the ball to me. I believe I can beat anyone on a post pattern. Of course, I couldn't do it without Hadl's perfect passes.

"Our balanced attack is also a big reason. Our opponents have had to stop our running game, and that has opened up our passing."

And when you're the fastest kid on the block and finally playing for a winner, the whole world opens up, too.

Index

INDEX

INDEX